HAUNTED BARABOO

HAUNTED BARABOO

SHELLEY MORDINI AND GWEN HERREWIG

Haunted America

Published by Haunted America
A Division of The History Press
Charleston, SC
www.historypress.com

Front cover: External view of the Al. Ringling Theatre in Downtown Baraboo. *Authors' collection.*
Back cover: Al. C. & Lou Ringling's Mausoleum in the Walnut Hill Cemetery. *Courtesy of Pam Thompson.*

Author photographs courtesy of Stephanie Shanks.

First published 2021

Manufactured in the United States

ISBN 9781467148368

Library of Congress Control Number: 2021938509

Notice: The information in this book is true and complete to the best of our knowledge. It is offered without guarantee on the part of the authors or The History Press. The authors and The History Press disclaim all liability in connection with the use of this book.

CONTENTS

Contents

ACKNOWLEDGEMENTS

A famous African proverb says it takes a village to raise a child. We found that it also takes a community to write a haunted book. We would like to thank the following people and businesses, without which we could not have successfully completed this journey.

- Peter Shrake from Circus World Museum's Robert L. Parkinson Library and Research Center, for supporting our project, listening to our ideas and letting us use photographs. Peter and this library is truly one of the hidden gems of Baraboo.
- Joe Ward, for his extensive work in documenting the history of Baraboo's downtown buildings. Thank you, also, to the Baraboo Public Library for having these volumes available online, which was a bonus for us, as a majority of this book was written during the COVID-19 pandemic.
- Darren Hornby and Ben Bromley from the Baraboo Area Chamber of Commerce, for sharing photographs, supporting our project and answering our numerous emails. These men help make Baraboo the "Greatest Place on Earth."
- Pam Thompson, Kandie Beckwith, Nellie Schmitz and Bill Johnsen, for allowing us to print images in our book. Thank you, also, to the businessowners and homeowners who took the time to talk to us and allowed us to take pictures.

- Our acquisitions editor, John Rodrigue, for his persistence and guidance.
- Stacie Heckendorf, Justin Strawther, Michelle Feld, Pierre Mordini, Mary Farrell-Stieve and Jennifer Redell, for reading versions of our stories and providing feedback.

Finally, a big thank-you to the more than forty-five people who shared their ghostly experiences with us. When we put out the call to collect stories, we weren't sure how many people would show up or if we would even have enough stories to fill a book. Well, in true Baraboo fashion, you all showed up with numerous stories and enthusiasm. We still get stopped on the streets by residents who say, "Aren't you the one who's writing that *Haunted Baraboo* book? Boy, do I have a story for you!" Keep stopping us—we enjoy each and every story. Email us at baraboottours@yahoo.com.

INTRODUCTION

The following stories feature detailed witness accounts of the spirits that put the *Boo* in Baraboo. Some ghosts are spooky tricksters, others seem to simply like the company of the living and a few are stuck in a loop of repetition, perpetually reenacting a scene from the past. A love of storytelling and ghost stories brought us together to write this book. Shelley is the owner of Baraboo Tours and started conducting haunted and historic downtown walks in Baraboo in 2011. Gwen is an experienced guide and has led haunted walks for many seasons.

Baraboo is a small city in south-central Wisconsin. A walk through the historic downtown district takes a person back to the late 1800s, when most of the buildings were built. Remodeling over the years has not diminished the authentic architectural appeal of the buildings, which gives Baraboo the feel of a Norman Rockwell painting. Seven circuses claim roots in Baraboo—the two largest being the Ringling Brothers World's Greatest Shows and their first cousins' circus, the Gollmar Brothers Greatest of American Shows. At one point, it was common in Baraboo to see elephants, giraffes and camels walking on the streets for their daily constitutional. Many areas in Baraboo are in the National Register of Historic Places and offer unique settings to modern-day hauntings.

This book includes haunted stories from Baraboo and the surrounding area. A few have been published before, but many have not. A number of these haunted tales were told to us by local residents over the years. All of the tales derive from historical facts, folklore and/or personal experiences.

Circus elephants walking on Ash Street, date unknown. *Courtesy of Kandie Beckwith.*

We conducted over forty-five interviews in an attempt to document firsthand witness accounts of ghosts in Baraboo. Many of these stories came to us from people who fall into all categories of belief—even those who don't believe in ghosts but cannot provide another explanation for what happened to them. Great time was taken to research individual stories in an attempt to include some historical context, and every effort was made to ensure historical accuracy. We relied on Joseph Ward's documentation of Baraboo's past in *Baraboo 1850–2010: Chronology of Growth of the Commercial & Retail Districts*, as well as other historical books, archived newspaper reports and magazine articles. It is not always easy to discern the origins of a spirit, and some remain a mystery.

When possible, the addresses of the buildings are included. In the case of private residences, only the street name is identified. Asterisks (*) are used behind names that have been changed for those who wanted to maintain their personal privacy. In writing, we were sensitive to the fact that some of the spirits are those of deceased relatives of current Baraboo residents, and therefore, the tales have not been dramatized or demonized. Not all ghost encounters make perfect stories for a book, and in some cases, little historical information could be found. We included some of these simpler short stories because, at some point, insignificant ghostly manifestations around town become significant if for no other reason than the sheer number of times they've been witnessed. We leave you, the reader, to decide what to make of these stories.

One need not look far to find ghost stories in Baraboo. Living in an area that is known to be haunted is like living in bear country; if you venture into it enough, you will eventually have an encounter. A person can learn a lot about the past by learning about who stuck around after death.

PART I

GHOSTS OF BARABOO'S DOWNTOWN HISTORIC DISTRICT

Oak Street in the Downtown Baraboo Historic District. *Courtesy of Bill Johnsen.*

1

Baraboo's Two Business Districts

There are two distinct business districts in downtown Baraboo: one is above the hill next to the Baraboo River, and the other is below the hill. Both appear to harbor their share of ghosts. Many of the remaining brick buildings in both districts were built in the 1870s and 1880s, and in some cases, they were not built until the 1930s. The Downtown Baraboo Historic District is situated above the hill, around the courthouse square, on the upper banks of the Baraboo River. It was constructed closer to the residential areas and took on commercial businesses such as storefronts, government offices, churches and banks. A fire in November 1878 burned down most of the original wooden buildings on Oak Street that faced the courthouse square. The remaining brick buildings were built after the fire and are well preserved. Seventy-five buildings in the Downtown Baraboo Historic District were added to the National Register of Historic Places in 2015.

The Southside Commercial District, below the hill on Walnut Street, between Water and Lynn Streets, was the early industrial district. This area was originally made up of mills, industry plants, breweries and grocery stores. Later, the railroad depot and the winter quarters of the Ringling Brothers Circus were the central focus of the area.

2

Old Baraboo Inn

135 Walnut Street

When a photograph of a ghost at the Old Baraboo Inn (OBI) was published on the front page of the *Baraboo News Republic* on October 31, 2003, owner B.C. Farr knew his secret was out. He had been in business for only two years, and the paranormal activity in the bar was hard to hide. Even nonbelievers had to admit there was something going on. Today, the Old Baraboo Inn is known as one of the most haunted saloons in Wisconsin. It has been featured in many books and numerous paranormal shows, including the Food Network's *10 Most Haunted Restaurants in America* and Travel Channel's *Hometown Horror.*

OBI is located in the Southside Commercial District of Baraboo, diagonally across from the old train depot. The charming brick building was originally opened as the Bender Hotel, with a saloon on the lower level and hotel on the upper. Mrs. Brandenburg, a mother to six children, sold her property to the Benders because it was slated to be sandwiched between two breweries in the mid-1860s. She moved her family to the north side of the river to get away from the atmosphere on the south side. Sauk County produced 2.7 million pounds of hops in 1867 alone, and Lynn Street was the up-and-coming location for breweries in Baraboo. The Bender Hotel, as well as the Miller-Bender Brewery next door, was operated by Anna Bender and her son after her husband, George, died in 1874. The brewery burned down in 1884. A tunnel beneath the road connected a different brewery to the basement of the Bender Hotel, making deliveries convenient. If you ask B.C., apparitions still use the tunnel between the two buildings, even though it was bricked up years ago.

An external view of the Old Baraboo Inn. *Courtesy of Pam Thompson.*

After the Bender family sold the building in the 1930s, a number of other businesses moved in before reopening as a bar called the OBI in 1962. Years later, B.C. bought the building a decade after it was partially destroyed by a fire in 1989. The building was in disrepair, but he felt like he belonged there. It wasn't until after he began renovating that he found out his parents met in the building in the 1940s, when it was Pierce's Café. His mother was a waitress, and his father worked at the nearby Effinger Brewery.

The more B.C. worked in the building, the more he felt like something was off. He saw things in his peripheral vision that vanished when he turned to look. Sometimes he'd hear voices, laughter and conversation from somewhere within the building. He would even hear his own name being called from time to time. When he'd arrive for work in the morning, his tools and other supplies were in different locations than they had been when he left. Thinking an intruder was coming into the building at night, he taped the windows and doors closed from the inside, but the seal was never broken. Finally, he concluded that he must be working too many hours and losing his mind.

With time, the ghosts got bolder and started moving things around downstairs while he worked upstairs. Then they began moving items that he was currently working with, like his hammer. He'd set it down to grab the next piece of wood, and it would be gone, only to show up again in the place he left it after walking downstairs to get another. The same type of thing happened to a man he hired to help him renovate. After blaming each other for leaving the lights on at night, even when they knew they had turned them off, they started to consider the idea that maybe a ghost was in the building.

So many uncanny things have happened inside the OBI that the stories included in this book are only a small sample of what happens in the bar. Full and partial apparitions, shadows, mists and orbs are common sightings. Cellphones and cameras take pictures by themselves. Keys, CDs, DVDs and notes disappear and then reappear. A bottle of Jack Daniels periodically flies off the shelf and smashes to the floor. Barstools move on their own or pile up in a pyramid in front of the door at night. The forces that move things within the building set the OBI apart from most other haunted places in Baraboo.

Once the word was out that the OBI was haunted, not all of its clientele embraced the idea. Many thought it was a gimmick to draw in more people. Even B.C. acknowledged that many of the stories were unbelievable, except that so many people had witnessed them. Whenever someone enters the bar saying they don't believe in ghosts, B.C. offers a word of caution. The

Barstools sometimes move on their own at the Old Baraboo Inn. *Courtesy of Pam Thompson.*

spirits often rise to the occasion and provide a personal ghostly encounter to nonbelievers, almost as if they want people to know they are there. He calls it "getting ghost bombed at the OBI." People enter as nonbelievers and leave as believers. OBI has changed hundreds of people's lives.

Early on, a nonbelieving friend of B.C.'s sat at the bar one afternoon and heard glass breaking in the kitchen. He yelled to B.C., asking if he had an angry dishwasher, but there wasn't anyone working in the kitchen at the time. B.C. ran over, opened the door and saw plates flying through the air. The plates flew at an upward angle, alternating between two piles—one on the countertop and the other by the door—then smashing against the wall above the dishwasher. Rattled, B.C. yelled at the unseen assailant, asserting that the plates were expensive, and then he stepped back out to the bar and closed the door. When the noise in the kitchen quieted, B.C. stepped back in to find broken glass everywhere. He shouted into the room again, "Well, this is a fine mess! Who is going to clean this up?" Then, unbelievably, a broom flew from the cabinet—straight up, like someone was holding it—and dropped on the broken glass at his feet.

A delivery man dropped off meat in the kitchen and mentioned that he didn't believe in ghosts. All of a sudden, he took off his hat, saying that he had been hit by something; then something hit him again. When he hastily retreated out the back door, a disembodied voice called after him, "Well, I'll see you, buddy."

Another salesman, after suggesting the ghosts were a promotional scam, saw the apparition of an old woman with long brown hair glare at him and then turn and walk into a wall. He returned only one time after that.

So, who is haunting the OBI? Many souls, it seems. All three levels of the OBI have paranormal activity. Spirits of women, children, cowboys and gangsters have all been encountered there at one time or another. Among the apparitions seen, a cowboy and an assumed prostitute called Mary are seen most often. The cowboy is tall and appears in a brown cowboy hat and vest. Mary has a feather in her long blond hair and wears a short red dress. She appears most often dancing when the song "The House Is Rockin'" by Stevie Ray Vaughan is played on the jukebox. To add to the mystery of Mary, an unknown man with an apparent sensitivity visited OBI years ago during a busy happy hour. He handed B.C. a note saying that he was there to help him with his "problem." The note listed the names of women who had, the man said, died in the building. Behind Mary's name, the note said that she had bled to death in 1903. Strangely enough, the jukebox number for "The House Is Rockin'" is 19/03.

Parents have found their kids playing with ghost children in the back room, having conversations and spinning with unseen entities at angles that could only be achieved while holding the hands of another child. Ghosts appear to try the same antics in the women's restroom with different customers. The toilets flush on their own, the lid from the garbage can flies across the room and, at times, the whole garbage can is placed in front of the stall door after someone enters. Previous employees of the building thanked B.C. for bringing the ghosts out into the open. Mary had been seen on a number of occasions, and past bartenders described her to a tee.

B.C. estimates that 95 percent of the energy in the OBI is good. Most of the ground and upper levels have what he describes as a "good party vibe." The basement, on the other hand, tends to be a bit darker, though he admits that the energy seems to move around a bit within the building. While renovating, B.C. found bullet holes in the walls of the bar area with the bullets still in them, suggesting, perhaps, that the history of the OBI might be a bit more sinister than what he originally thought. A support pole in the basement also has bullet holes at head and stomach level.

The basement consists of a number of small rooms, hallways with dirt floors and a section that looks to have been finished off as a speakeasy during Prohibition (1920–1933) when the sale, manufacture and transportation of alcoholic beverages was illegal in the United States. The name *speakeasy* originated from patrons speaking quietly in order to avoid raising suspicion about illicit drinks. The basement of the OBI would have been a good location for this type of activity since there were three exits: through the tunnel, up through the bar or directly to the parking lot. A district judge ordered that the doors of the restaurant be padlocked for one year in 1929 as a result of a raid that occurred on the property. Many raids and arrests were made in Baraboo at the time for illicit alcohol sales.

Rumors have persisted that the building was a brothel at one point and even hosted occasional mobsters. Its proximity to the railroad tracks and breweries makes these claims plausible for some, but no hard evidence has been found to support them. That's not to say the idea is impossible. Gangster sightings, at the time, were printed in local newspapers. The sisters at the St. Mary's Ringling Hospital unwittingly hosted John Dillinger at a mass in 1934, after they noticed him holding a rosary on the property during their benediction. They were surprised to see his picture in the newspaper the next morning, identifying him as a wanted criminal.

Most of the time, the ghostly encounters in the basement are playful, but sometimes, people get hurt or scared. Bartenders have gone down to

The stairs that lead to the basement at the Old Baraboo Inn. *Courtesy of Pam Thompson.*

grab beer out of the walk-in cooler and have struggled to get out after the door closed behind them and the light turned off on its own. But not all encounters in the basement have been bad. One bartender was apparently caught in midair on the basement stairs after falling backward while carrying up cases of beer.

B.C. has had a few notable experiences, too. A large orb flew through the bar and hit him in the elbow with such force that it launched his whole body around and hyperextended his elbow. Another time, a helium balloon from St. Patrick's Day chased him through the bar. He had placed it in a hutch to get it off the counter, and almost immediately, the balloon lowered itself out of the hutch and then flew back over to him. The weight at the bottom of the string, which held the balloon down, remained suspended in the air. He backed up, and the balloon followed him along the bar, then around the other side of the bar, through the back room and all the way around the pool table. When B.C. returned to the bar, where the whole thing started, he stabbed the balloon with a pen.

For anyone wanting to get in on the action, a furnished, two-bedroom haunted suite is available to rent on the second floor. A man stayed there one night, and just as he was getting up to go to bed, an unusual pressure on his chest caused him to hesitate for a moment, right as the light fixture fell from the ceiling, barely missing his head. It came down with such force that the threads pulled through the nut, and the wires were ripped out of the ceiling. The light crashed to the floor in a spectacular shower of sparks. The incident blew the breaker, and the room went dark. The man called from the sidewalk at 1:00 a.m. and had to be talked into going back upstairs because all of the other hotels in town were booked.

3

126 Third Street

Not all ghosts are able to make their presence known as dramatically as others, and sometimes, they wouldn't behave poorly, even if they could. But if a ghost wants to alter the way in which they are portrayed on a guided tour, they are left with the arduous task of finding a way to communicate. This appears to be what happened at the Con Amici Craft Bar in downtown Baraboo.

The building was originally known as the Luther Saloon. Tragedy, combined with a lifetime of dedication to a family business, appears to have resulted in the spirit of at least one owner still haunting the Con Amici Craft Bar, though few people notice them eavesdropping on conversations. In fact, no one has ever actually seen an apparition in the building, but plenty of people sense the presence. Co-owner Nellie Schmitz reports feeling like she is being watched on a regular basis, particularly in the center of the building, near the bathroom.

Chicago native John Luther relocated to Baraboo in 1881 and bought the newly erected brick building on Third Street, which replaced James Cowles's Blacksmith Shop after a fire collapsed a shared wall. John Luther opened the John F. Luther Saloon, a fine establishment with an upright piano, spittoons lining the floor and gas light fixtures hanging from a decorative tin ceiling. He offered a variety of cigars to his patrons, a lunch buffet and a plethora of drinks.

A view of Luther Saloon from the front of the building, date unknown. *Courtesy of the Con Amici Craft Bar.*

Perhaps less talked about was a "tearoom" in the back where women gathered, since they were not allowed in the main bar. Historical photographs portray the tearoom, known as the Luther Palm Garden, as having a feminine touch with a slight Mediterranean feel, wooden tables and tall palms positioned throughout. During renovations in 2012, workers pulled down drywall and found the original murals, which continue to decorate the walls today. The murals are thought to have been painted by Joe Hitcherson, an artist who painted scenes on Ringling Brothers Circus wagons. Even to the casual observer, there are uncanny similarities between the Con Amici Craft Bar of today and the John F. Luther Saloon of the late 1800s. The general layout of the two establishments is almost identical. Even the tile floor, which William Luther installed in 1904, after taking over his father's bar, is still visible.

John Luther's sons, Otto and William Luther, joined their father in the daily operations of the bar as soon as they were old enough. On June 30, 1896, no one at the Luther Saloon could have foreseen the catastrophe that was about to unfold. The gas lighting in the building was problematic. When the smell of gas wafted through the saloon from the back of the building, John and his son Otto immediately abandoned the lunch buffet, which they had been organizing for a number of patrons, and ran to find the source. Joseph Ward described what happened next in volume 5 of *Baraboo Wisconsin 1850 to 2010*:

> *The son led the way to a rear room, mounted a stepladder, and struck a match to determine where the leak might be. The gas was very dense near the ceiling and no sooner had he lit the match than the explosion took place. The young man's clothes took fire, and all that was left of his shirt and vest were just a few fragments. He was severely burned from his head down as far as his waist and was in great agony. John Luther…was also severely burned about the face, back, and hands. When the flames accompanying the explosion burst forth, the visitors in the saloon rushed for the street, and for a time, the wildest excitement prevailed.*

Otto died of his injuries the next day, July 1, 1896, one day before his eighteenth birthday. His father survived the ordeal. Four years after Otto's death, John's son William took over the saloon and changed its name to

The palm garden in the back room of Luther Saloon, date unknown. *Courtesy of the Con Amici Craft Bar.*

William F. Luther, Sample Rooms. He kept the bar through the beginning of Prohibition, converting it into a bowling alley and soft drink parlor, but he likely kept a stash of booze in the basement, as was common at the time. William sold the building in 1928, and it would house a number of shops before reverting back to a bar in 2012.

Local resident Jenea Sailing visited the Con Amici Craft Bar (then called the Con Amici Wine Bar) on August 4, 2017. She sat with a friend, shoulder to the bar, eyes drawn to the back of the room. Something was telling her to go there. Jenea had a sensitivity; she could communicate with spirits, but it was a secret that she was not completely comfortable with—at least, not yet. She tried to ignore it, but the pull was too strong and distracting.

An hour later, she made eye contact with a tour guide who sat in the back of the room after completing a haunted walk of downtown Baraboo. Jenea had never felt such a strong draw to a person she had never met before and went over to find out why. The guide confirmed that the Con Amici had a known spirit attached to it. However, the guide did not disclose the fact that she, personally, did not believe the Con Amici to be haunted. The guide often omitted the story of Otto's death from her tours in favor of other more colorful stories from around town, except on the occasion someone from her group ventured off to the bathroom alone. Jenea did not want to hear the ghost story. Instead, she wanted to tell the guide the information she received from the spirit, and in exchange, the guide agreed to tell her whether or not she was crazy.

Jenea immediately started by describing a picture of the spirit that she received in her head. "It's a man," she said, "in the 1920s. I see wing-tipped shoes. He is wearing a suit, jacket, and a hat. I sense he is here all the time. He wants everyone to know this is still his bar."

The guide froze. Unbeknownst to Jenea, a historical photograph of the Luther Saloon hung nearby on the wall. The guide often pointed it out on her tours. In it, three men stood at the bar. One wore a suit and hat, similar to the man Jenea described. But maybe everyone did back then.

Jenea continued, "He likes the music and the people that come here. His name is William."

Jenea then sat back in her chair as the spirit seemed to trigger an overwhelming heat that engulfed her body. She swept a hand from her head to her right leg, showing where the heat was most intense. The guide immediately interpreted that this represented the burns that Otto endured from the explosion and told Jenea so. Jenea received validation from more than one spirit, confirming that they had gotten the story right. The spirit

An interior view of the Luther Saloon from the rear of the building, date unknown. *Courtesy of the Con Amici Craft Bar.*

even went so far as to relay that, when he died, he saw a light similar to the overexposed part of the historical photograph.

The guide took Jenea to the back room where the original murals are visible from the era of Luther's Palm Garden and explained the significance of the "tearoom" as a place where women gathered, since they weren't allowed in the main bar. Jenea received an image of a woman pulling a flask from her stockings, and the spirit assured them that the women drank plenty. Jenea's attention immediately focused to the front-left side of the room, where the explosion had occurred. She then focused on the murals and said, "He comes back here to remember his life. This is where he feels most at home."

Suddenly, a large lightbulb overhead began to flicker dramatically. As the spirit drew Jenea's attention to it, she asked him to stop if he was responsible. Within a couple of seconds, the flickering slowed and then stopped completely. He had physically established his presence—if there was still any question at this point.

Jenea relayed a message to the guide from the spirit, and suddenly, the strong draw she detected in the beginning between the spirit and the guide became clear; he was not able to communicate with the guide himself. Jenea

An interior view of the back room at the Con Amici Craft Bar, showing the old murals painted for the Palm Garden. *Courtesy of Pam Thompson.*

relayed that the spirit always got the feeling that the guide didn't really believe he was there, and he hoped that with this new information, she would be able to incorporate what she had learned into a better story about him on her tours. The guide agreed. The fact that the content of her haunted tour was being criticized by a ghost was not lost on the guide.

4

WRIGHT BUILDING

CORNER OF OAK AND FOURTH STREETS

This cream-colored brick building was built by businesswoman Elizabeth Wright in 1881, after a fire on November 6, 1878, burned down much of the block on Oak Street. The name Wright can still be seen on a nameplate on the upper side of the front of the building. The Wright Building is quite large compared to many other buildings in downtown Baraboo. It was designed to accommodate four storefronts on the street level and a number of well-lit offices on the second story, with an eighteen-foot-wide hallway in the middle. On occasion, businessowners in the upper level of the Wright Building find themselves walking the dark hallways in the evening, trying to figure out who is in the building with them. Many have experienced disembodied voices or footsteps, as well as unexplained sounds and movements.

It is unclear whether the activity in the Wright Building is from the years of business operations within the building or if it is left over from the hotel that previously stood on the property. A hotel called the Adam's House, one of the first hotels in the area, originally stood on this site and was built in 1847 as a one-story wooden structure. By 1854, it was expanded to three-stories, with balconies on all levels, and then renamed the Western Hotel. The hotels in Baraboo became busy with the arrival of the railroad in 1871. Mary Todd Lincoln, the widow of Abraham Lincoln, stayed at the Western Hotel in 1872, seven years after Lincoln's assassination.

August Reinking purchased the Wright Building in 1899 and opened a dry goods store on the street level, which remained in operation through

An external view of the Wright Building. *Courtesy of Pam Thompson.*

multiple generations until the 1980s. Many other businesses in the building came and went throughout the years. The Ringling Brothers Circus rented rooms on the second story sometime around 1901 for a wardrobe department, which was directed by Lou Ringling (Al. Ringling's wife). The main sewing rooms were in the upper front corner of the building. It is rumored that Lou arranged for the installation of the bay window that still overlooks Fourth Street in order to display circus costumes created by her talented seamstresses. Sensitives who have visited the second floor of the building have picked up on a festive atmosphere in the hallways, with circus performers and families coming and going and even parties to celebrate the end of the season.

Since 2012, Karmen Linder has had a photography studio in the same office as the old Ringling wardrobe department. She was working on paperwork one Sunday afternoon in the fall, after everyone had left for the day. The building was quiet. Her desk backed up to a locked adjoining door to another photography studio next door, which was seldom used. Suddenly, she heard a loud crash coming from the other side of the door. Karmen envisioned the chandelier crashing to the floor at the beginning of the *Phantom of the Opera*. It sounded as though parts shattered all over, hitting the door and walls. The glass would have flooded into her office under the door if she hadn't had a draft stopper in place for privacy. All she could think was that maybe the studio lights had fallen over. She went into the hallway, straining to see into the studio from the office window, but she wasn't able to see anything because of the layout of the room. The next day, she waited and intercepted the studio owner as he arrived. She told him that something had shattered inside his shop, but he laughed and said that was impossible. He didn't have any lights back there, and the floor was carpeted, so a crash as she described was impossible. Still, Karmen followed him into the studio, and sure enough, nothing had fallen. The room was spotless. That is when she learned the building was haunted and that things like that happened all the time.

On many afternoons, when the building is quiet, Karmen hears a faint party. The party sounds old-fashioned and reminds her of what it might have been like to hear a black-tie party in first class from the lower second-class level of the *Titanic*. The festivities sound like they might be coming

Employees working in the Ringling Brothers Circus wardrobe department on Water Street in 1913. The wardrobe department was once in the upper level of the Wright Building. *Courtesy of Circus World/Wisconsin Historical Society.*

through the vents—except they aren't. It's a cocktail party or a celebration, and she can't make out what people are saying, only that there is a lot of chatter, little cheers and excitement. She often opens the door and peeks her head out into the hallway; sometimes, she even puts her ear up to other office doors to try and figure out where it is coming from, but she has never found the source.

Every once in a while, Karmen's clients have ghostly experiences in the middle of photography sessions, and it makes her nervous. She is afraid something might happen beyond her control, and she doesn't want that to reflect negatively on her business. One day, a father sat on the couch and mentioned that he suddenly became chilled. Karmen immediately thought she had a presence in the room. He then said he felt the hair standing up on the back of his neck. Whenever something like this happens, Karmen stops the shoot and asks everyone to look around the room and comment on how beautiful it is. She explains a bit of the history about the room—how it was the wardrobe department for the circus—and asks them to focus on the creativity in the room and all of the colors. They flood the room with audible compliments, and that seems to make the spirit happy. On this particular day, one of the shutters that Karmen uses as a prop lifted off the wall and bumped back without being touched. Then everything went back to normal.

Ken Parker managed Von Klaus Winery for four of the fifteen years that it was located on the second floor of the Wright Building, before it moved to its current location on Third Avenue. The winery was at the top of the ramp, which leads away from the lower wardrobe department area. The ramp was made of wood, and it made distinct thuds and creaky noises as people walked up and down. Late in the evening, Ken heard people walking up and down the ramp, even when he knew he was the only person in the building and the hallway had been dark for hours. One night in the fall of 2016, he stayed to work late in the back office and heard two children giggling in the hallway. The sound came from the lower area, down the ramp. Thinking this was strange, he went out to see what the children were doing in the dark hallway, but the lights were off in all of the office windows, and he was alone.

Kristen Philipp, the owner of Seek Boutique, rented a couple of offices on the second floor of the Wright Building before moving to her current location on Fourth Street. She first opened her business in an office space up the ramp and stayed well after midnight, tagging items with a friend. At around 1:30 a.m., the smell of perfume engulfed the room. It was strong

Shutters from the Karmen Linder Photography Studio. A shutter once moved on its own. *Courtesy of Pam Thompson.*

and similar to a scent that an older woman might wear. Then, two minutes later, a disembodied male voice asked, "You girls want some popcorn?" It sounded like it had come from miles away, but at the same time, it was totally clear, as if it were right next to their ears. They declined the popcorn and left for the evening.

Another time, a gentleman approached Kristen and another employee at the counter, acknowledging that what he was about to say sounded strange. He could clearly see only two women standing at the counter, but there were three women in the reflection in the window behind them.

Kristen moved her business to a second location, next to Karmen Linder Photography, in the room where Karmen had previously heard the massive crash years before. One night, Kristen saw her antique floor lamp swinging back and forth in the back of the room; it was swinging with such force that it should have fallen over. It eventually slowed and stopped. Shaken, she removed the lamp from the shop and placed it outside the door, where a guide and patrons from Baraboo Tours witnessed the same lamp swinging back and forth during a haunted tour of the building.

5
119 Third Avenue

Michael Yount, the owner of Tin Roof Dairy, is a skeptic when it comes to ghosts, but he cannot deny witnessing a number of strange things during his first year of business. The bell on the front door dings on its own, the sound of footsteps can be heard on the roof when no one is up there and a musical carousel once played music, even though it had been spun out for months.

The two-story brick building was built in 1872. Although originally opened as "The Deutscher Store," two businesses are long known to have occupied the space. In 1886, William Stanley expanded his grocery business next door to include 119 Third Avenue. For decades, the Stanleys sold groceries and dried goods. The upstairs area of the building was known as "Stanley Hall" and housed such organizations as the Masonic Lodge in 1885 and a millinery, and in the late 1920s, it was home to the YWCA. After forty-eight years of business, the Gamble Corporation bought the building in 1934 and operated a Gamble Store until 1984, selling everything from hardware, housewares and plumbing and heating goods to automotive needs, appliances and farm supplies.

In 2019, Michael opened Tin Roof Dairy, an old-fashioned ice cream parlor with a 1930s bar, a Wurlitzer jukebox and an 1880s-era photograph of a man standing in front of the building when it was identified as the Stanley Company. He installed a set of bells above the door to notify staff when new customers arrived. The bells ring hundreds of times per day as the door is opened and closed. But about twice per week, the bell rings

A musical carousel that played music on its own. *Courtesy of Pam Thompson.*

on its own, without anyone being near the door. Wanting to find a logical explanation, Michael and his staff opened and closed the door a number of times, thinking that it must have been stuck, maybe the wind blew it open or whatever theory they tried to use as an explanation. They have never been able to recreate a scenario in which the door bumps the bells or the bells ring on their own. This, by itself, was no reason to think the building was haunted, but it has caused considerable puzzlement among the staff.

Then, on three separate occasions, Michael heard distinct footsteps overhead while he was working in the back room. They quickly walked across the roof, from west to east. The building has high ceilings, and the only access to the roof was through an upstairs apartment, which no one was living in. The first two times he heard footsteps, he thought about it and wondered how it was possible. The third time, he dropped everything he was doing, ran up the stairs to the apartment and unlocked the door, only to find the apartment empty. The source of the footsteps remains unsolved.

So, when a musical carousel suddenly began spinning and playing music on a shelf, Michael immediately wondered if it was a coincidence or a ghost. The few patrons in the shop looked at their phones, thinking the music was a ringtone. When no one had any calls or texts, they followed the sound to find the carousel rotating on the shelf fifteen feet away. It stopped about thirty seconds later—as quickly as it started.

Since the staff has been unable to find logical explanations for these events, they have begun attributing all unexplained experiences to the man in the historic photograph on the wall, which still overlooks the dairy. They call him Stanley for lack of any other name. Although it is unknown whether the photograph actually shows Stanley or someone else, it does appear that something uncanny is happening at Tin Roof Dairy.

6
420 OAK STREET

Although the current owners of Neat-O's Bake Shoppe have not had any ghostly encounters at this location, a previous baker had an unexpected visit from spirits that seemed to originate from a saloon that operated at this site from 1885 to 1891. The building was built in 1878 as a billiard hall, but a fire destroyed the interior within two years of opening. A number of different businesses came and went over the years until it opened as a bakery in the 1990s.

The baker lived in the apartment upstairs, which made his early-morning arrivals convenient. One morning, he rolled out of bed at 4:00 a.m. to start baking. Bleary-eyed, he went downstairs and began turning on the lights. When he reached the front area of the bakery, he saw four women floating

An external view of Neat-O's Bake Shoppe. *Courtesy of Pam Thompson.*

in the air, as if they were being projected out of the mirrors behind them. They were dressed as old-time barmaids. Behind them, he clearly saw an old-fashioned saloon with an ornate bar and a brass boot rail along the bottom. A large spittoon sat on the floor at the end of the bar. He could hear upbeat piano music but couldn't see the instrument. The women were laughing, dancing and kicking up their legs in time to the music. One woman turned and made eye contact with him, then reached out her ghostly arm toward him. He screamed and stepped back. Then the whole scene vanished. All of the hairs on his arms stood up with the energy in the air. He rubbed his eyes, trying to judge if what he had just witnessed was real. With a shaky laugh, the baker spoke to the empty room, "You are welcome to use this space any time I am not here, but *please* do not show yourselves again." That was the last time he saw the dancing girls.

7

University of Wisconsin–Platteville at Baraboo Sauk County

Connie Road

In a town like Baraboo that already has a *boo* in its name, it's not hard to imagine how the local college came up with their mascot, the Fighting Spirits. The campus, now known as University of Wisconsin (UW)–Platteville at Baraboo Sauk County, opened in 1968 with a lot of pomp and circumstance. Three elephants from Circus World Museum joined in the groundbreaking ceremony to give the event a Baraboo flair. The original campus consisted of three buildings: a student center and administration office, a library and a classroom building. The student senate hung a sign outside the library on the first day of school, saying, "Welcome to Boo-U." The nickname Boo-U has stuck ever since.

Officially, the campus has no ghosts. Unofficially, the students of the theater department have wondered if the theater is haunted, though it is impossible to figure out who or what might be responsible for the haunting. In 2012, Drake Lewerenz took a work study position as an assistant to the theater director. His main job was to keep the theater organized. He cleaned the dressing rooms and organized the costume closet and lighting rooms. The costume closet was a cavernous room under the stage that served, for a time, as a green room where performers relaxed when not performing. At the time, the area had the rusty remnants of a shower, missing ceiling tiles, water stains, ancient carpeting and an ominous doorway that led to the boiler room. The space was not comfortable to be in, especially alone. One day, when Drake was in the costume area, folding bolts of fabric for the

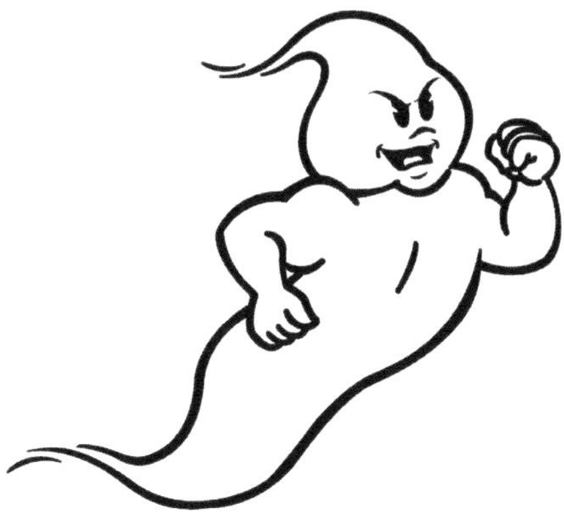

The Baraboo Fighting Spirits mascot. *Courtesy of UW–Platteville at Baraboo Sauk County.*

stage, the room grew noticeably still. From the depths of the nearby boiler room came the sound of a baby crying. He froze and listened intently, trying to rationalize the existence of the sound. After a few minutes of hearing the intense wailing, Drake bolted out of the basement, not even bothering to shut off the lights on his way out. In the four years that Drake attended Boo-U, he never went back near the boiler room area with its inky blackness.

Rebecca Hassebrock attended Boo-U from September 2016 to August 2018. She also took a work study position as the assistant to the theater director. Rebecca spent a lot of time down in the costume area, cleaning and straightening up. She described her ghostly experiences as feeling a presence in the costume closet and a general sense of being watched. Goosebumps, chills and unease were common emotions for Rebecca to feel while working there. One time, Rebecca had an unusual incident with the elevator. She heard the elevator go upstairs as if it had been called by someone. It returned to the basement, and the door opened as if to let someone off the elevator, but no one was there. Rebecca suspected at the time that no one alive got off the elevator, but some unknown spirit was coming down to get a costume. To try to make her workspace friendlier, Rebecca started to greet the room when entering to make sure that no one else was there and to let the spirits know that she was coming in.

8

Baraboo Civic Center

124 Second Street

The origin of a haunting is often difficult to discern. The Baraboo Civic Center has had thousands of people come and go throughout the years. It was built in 1928 and originally served as the high school for Baraboo, but it wasn't the first school at this location. The block of Second and Oak Streets has been the location of several schools since 1860. The first high school burned on February 9, 1906, around 11:30 a.m., while school was in session, but all three hundred students managed to evacuate without injury. A new, redbrick high school was built in its place but was already too small by 1927, when plans were underway to build an additional building.

The school board hired architectural firm Claude and Starck from Madison, Wisconsin, to build the new high school. Partner Louis Claude grew up in Baraboo in a house at Devils Lake, near the north shore. Claude and Starck designed the high school in the Prairie style, which was influenced by Frank Lloyd Wright, among others. It also displays hints of Gothic, Arts and Crafts and other styles that were popular at the time, which gives the building a particularly haunted feel. Pairs of griffins, mythical creatures with the heads and wings of eagles and the bodies of lions, still decorate the three entrances. By 1928 standards, the new school was very modern, with electric lights wired in all of the rooms, telephones connecting various departments and a system of call bells operated by an electric clock in the office. The older redbrick high school remained next door and became the middle school, and the two were connected by a tunnel that, in part, can still be seen today on the west side of the building.

An exterior view of the former Baraboo High School, date unknown. *Courtesy of Kandie Beckwith.*

Griffins at the entrance of the Baraboo Civic Center. *Authors' collection.*

The building became the Baraboo Civic Center in 1962, when it, again, became too small, and the current high school was built on Draper Street. The Baraboo Civic Center is now home to the Boys and Girls Club and the Baraboo Parks and Recreation Department. Office space is also available for rent.

It is in one of these rented offices that Jerry Miller* claims to have had a ghost encounter. Jerry rented an office with a glass door leading to the hallway. One afternoon in May, Jerry was working at his desk and noticed something out of the corner of his eye. As he turned toward the door, he saw a large, smoky orb in the hallway. It seemed to drift to the left, then to the right and then it moved slowly toward the door before dissipating. Within five minutes, the entire room got very cold—to the point that he could see his breath. Jerry called maintenance to come and examine the air register in the room, but everything appeared normal with the system. The room remained noticeably colder for twenty minutes before returning to a normal temperature. One may never know if this ghostly encounter was a former student or principal, but it was nice of the spirit to provide air conditioning on a hot day.

9

Ghost Train

Train Depot on Lynn Street

The idea of a ghost train visiting Baraboo is not a new one. For decades, residents near the old train station at the Walnut Street crossing have joked about a ghost train. On occasion, the crossing lights signal that a train is coming, and the gate lowers, but no train comes. Residents wait in their cars, and neighborhood children run to the end of their yards, looking for the train. The gate eventually goes back up, and the lights stop flashing.

A tavern owner near the old depot attributes an occasional uptick in ghostly activity in the bar to the ghost train. He claims that the spirits of gamblers, cowboys and circus performers arrive every month or so on the ghost train and spend their layovers there. The gambler has been captured in photographs; he sits at the bar and has his sleeves rolled up.

The first train arrived in Baraboo on September 12, 1871. It was a moment of pride for the city because it had tried, unsuccessfully, for over twenty years to get the train to come to town. There was so much excitement around the arrival of the first train that it was met with a welcoming committee, an enormous arch and young women in white dresses who decorated the engine with flags, flowers, berries, streamers and garland. A depot was constructed on Lynn Street, then replaced with a larger brick structure, which is still standing today. On the other side of Walnut Street, across from the Old Baraboo Inn, a roundhouse and turntable once stood. By 1905, one in eight Baraboo residents worked for the railroad, and a double track was installed to accommodate additional traffic. The second story of the depot was home to the Chicago & North Western Railroad Division's headquarters.

Left: The railroad tracks at the Walnut Street crossing, where some people claim a ghost train arrives. *Courtesy of Bill Johnsen.*

Below: The Chicago and North Western depot, date unknown. *Courtesy of Kandie Beckwith.*

The train depot is currently owned and being renovated by the Sauk County Historical Society, but in its heyday, the depot was a busy place, with up to eighteen passenger trains per day and fifty freight trains. Travelers frequently had layovers in Baraboo, and the boardinghouses were full. Train whistles blew day and night throughout the city. Each train tooted twenty times as it went through—four toots at each of the five railroad crossings. A former railroad worker named Frank worked for the passenger trains as a baggage boy when he was young, and every time he heard the train whistle blow, he thought to himself, "Money, Money, Money." Money did flow into Baraboo. A 1909 rate schedule listed the monthly salary for a brakeman and flagman as $62.50, and engineers received $144.40.

Eventually, the need for the rail line diminished with the invention of automobiles. The last passenger train left Baraboo in 1963, and the freight office closed in 1984. The track west of Reedsburg was also abandoned. Today, the Baraboo portion of track is still used but with greatly limited service—except for the ghost train.

10

Van Orden Mansion

531 Fourth Avenue

The Sauk County Historical Museum is a mansion originally built by Jacob Van Orden, and only the Van Orden family has lived in it. The mansion has been under the control of the Sauk County Historical Society since 1938, when Jacob's daughter-in-law sold it for $9,000, which was less than the cost to build it. It is now open to the public, and visitors are delighted by a sense of going back in time to the early 1900s. The house has its original light fixtures, furniture, woodwork and flooring. Even the original maids' and butlers' pantries are still intact. The building is said to have a spirit that causes unexplained noises throughout the house.

In 1874, when Jacob Van Orden landed a job at the Bank of Baraboo (now the Baraboo State Bank) as a general utility clerk, few people could have guessed that, by 1902, he would be in a position to build a fourteen-room mansion. He was eighteen years old in 1874 and had just moved to Baraboo. His main duties were to sweep out the bank and run errands. Within five years, he became a cashier, and over the next thirty years, he became an influential employee at the bank.

Jacob worked closely with the Ringling brothers as they attempted to start their circus. In 1885, the Bank of Baraboo provided a loan of one hundred dollars, with 8 percent interest, for the startup costs of their circus, which the brothers promptly repaid. Each year after, the bank approved higher and higher loans for the circus, and in time, the deposits from the circus enhanced the status of the bank, as the Ringling brothers became wealthy.

An external view of the Van Orden Mansion. *Courtesy of Pam Thompson.*

By 1902, Jacob's social and economic status had reached a point that warranted a new house. He hired the prestigious Milwaukee architectural firm Ferry & Clas to design and build a Tudor Revival–style mansion. It cost $10,000 and was completed in 1903. It was a cutting-edge mansion at the time, boasting gas and electric lighting, indoor plumbing, five fireplaces, marble sinks and a third-story ballroom.

In 1915, at the age of fifty-nine, Jacob became the president of the bank. Jacob was also an active member in the community, a thirty-second-degree Mason, and he was known to make liberal contributions for historical and archaeological preservation. He died in 1927 at the age of seventy-one.

At one point through the years, the historical society used the mansion as its main office, and that's when staff began noticing unexplained sounds in the house. Carl Smith* worked with the Sauk County Historical Society at the Van Orden Mansion for nine years. He conducted administrative work, research and guided tours. His desk was on the first floor, in the living room, and he frequently heard someone walking upstairs, even when there was no one else in the building. The footsteps were casual and not loud, heavy or fast. They were puzzling because another employee had an office on the second floor (at the end of the hallway in the original maid's room), but Carl wasn't able to hear his coworker walk up the stairs or down the hallway.

In fact, the sound of the footsteps could not be replicated anywhere in the house. The employee upstairs also heard the footsteps on occasion, but he thought they were coming from the attic. Sometimes, one of them but not the other would hear the footsteps. There were times when they both heard the footsteps, but no matter their location in the house, the footsteps always sounded like they were coming from overhead.

About once a month, Carl and his coworker would hear a loud bang in the house, as if a large piece of furniture had fallen over. An extensive search of the entire house never revealed anything out of place. His coworker, trying to find a rational explanation, suggested that perhaps a weight in one of the windows had rotted and fell off inside the wall. But it never sounded like it came from a window.

They began assigning responsibility for the strange noises to Viola Putz, a twenty-eight-year-old maid who died suddenly in 1937. She had been working for Jacob's son Lucas and his wife, Florence, for nine years. Sometime during the summer of 1937, she began feeling sick, but the condition did not appear serious until it abruptly worsened, and she was transported to the hospital. She died two days later. Rumors flew through town about the possible reasons for her death, but her obituary mentions nothing about it.

Of course, no one knows for sure whether or not Viola Putz is responsible for the unexplained sounds in the Van Orden Mansion, but witnesses standing outside the mansion have reported seeing the curtains move in the upper window, as if someone was looking out to see who had arrived. The mansion was closed at the time, but even if someone were in the house, the window is located behind a large display case, and the curtain would be nearly impossible to reach—unless the person were able to walk through furniture.

PART II

CIRCUS SPIRITS

11
KEEPING THE CIRCUS SPIRIT ALIVE

If having a town full of circus workers results in freak-show hauntings, then Baraboo, home of the Ringling Brothers and Gollmar Brothers Circuses, should be teeming with them. In fact, some departed circus animals and workers have been known to emerge from time to time, and a number of circus-related hauntings have been reported over the years. Shortly after a local resident purchased a vanity from a vintage resale store in Baraboo, ghostly clowns began appearing in the background of photographs that she took around her home. The first ghostly clown image showed up in the mirror of the vanity, and the second was in the window of a home she had just purchased. She sold the vanity soon after.

In his book *Paranormal Wisconsin Dells and Baraboo*, Chad Lewis reports that as far back as December 1953, *Fate Magazine* ran a story about phantom elephants ramming into a house on Eighth Street, rattling the windows and demolishing an old barn in the backyard. The incident also involved a police cruiser being pushed uphill when no one was looking and the distinct odor of large, dirty animals. The article referenced a newspaper article from 1930 as the original source for the story, but at the time of this writing, the original article had not been found to substantiate the claim.

Salome and August Ringling had eight children, seven of whom were involved in the circus at one time or another. Although Baraboo is known as the hometown of the Ringling Brothers Circus, the Ringlings did not live in Baraboo permanently until 1875. August was a harness maker and moved the family frequently, looking for profitable work, but the family often

Ringling Brothers Circus performers inside the big top tent in 1887. Lou Ringling is seated in the front right. *Courtesy of Circus World/Wisconsin Historical Society.*

lived in dismal poverty. On May 19, 1884, the Ringling Brothers Circus performed its first tent show on an empty lot in Baraboo, on the corner of Broadway Street and Second Avenue. In the beginning, Al. and his brothers made up most of the show. They would go on to create one of the largest circuses in America. Even after reaching fame, they continued to winter in Baraboo each year, storing their wagons and exotic animals on Water Street, near the Baraboo River (now Circus World Museum).

The general opinion at the time was that a circus wasn't a real circus until it had an elephant. The Ringlings were able to purchase their first two elephants in 1888. By the winter of 1910, they were housing thirty-seven elephants at their winter quarters. Elephants are still used in circus performances at Circus World Museum. While no aggressive phantom elephant encounters have been reported in the last half century, some Baraboo residents claim to hear trumpeting elephants, sometimes in the winter, near Circus World Museum, even though there are no elephants there in the winter.

The Gollmar brothers, first cousins of the Ringling brothers, also ran a circus out of Baraboo called the Gollmar Brothers Greatest of American

Elephants began wintering with the circus in Baraboo in 1888. *Courtesy of Bill Johnsen.*

Ringling family portrait. (*Back, left to right*) Al., Alf T., Gus, Charles and Otto. (*Front, left to right*) John; Marie Salome Juliar, mother; August, father; Ida, sister; and Henry. Date unknown. *Courtesy of the Baraboo Chamber of Commerce.*

Shows. The five Gollmar brothers, Walter, Fred, Charles, Ben and Jake, wintered in Baraboo (on Second Avenue) from 1891 to 1916 and always staged a street parade in downtown Baraboo before leaving on tour for the season. The Ringling and Gollmar brothers' first cousins Henry and Corwin Moeller ran a wagon shop in Baraboo and built cage and baggage wagons for the circuses as well as many of the decorative circus wagons.

Circus parades were common during the peak of traveling circuses. On arriving in a new community, while workers erected the tents and other things that were needed for performances, the rest of the crew paraded their elaborately decorated wagons, wild animals and performers through the downtown streets to attract publicity and customers. It gave the community a taste of what was in store—if they attended the show. While opening Circus World Museum in 1959, Chappie Fox had a vision to stage an old-fashioned circus parade as a promotional feat to show off the museum's collection of antique circus wagons. As a result, the Great Circus Parade was organized thirty times between 1963 and 2010,

A circus parade in downtown Baraboo, date unknown. *Courtesy of Kandie Beckwith.*

A photograph showing "666" in the sky, taken on the weekend of the Circus Celebration, 2019. *Courtesy of Audrey Tracy.*

mostly in Milwaukee, Wisconsin, and a few times in Chicago, Illinois, and Baraboo, Wisconsin.

In mid-July 2012, Baraboo began an annual Big Top Parade and Circus Celebration, which honors the memory of Baraboo's circus history. The event brings thirty thousand people to town, some of whom are current or former circus performers. Clowns, circus wagons and stilt walkers line the street. Strangely, local haunted guides claim to experience an occasional uptick in paranormal activity, often in the form of something playful, while hosting annual tours for former clowns. On one occasion, a guest captured a picture of (apparent) swirling orbs in the sky that resulted in the numbers 666 appearing. Of course, a logical explanation, such as a trick of the light, could explain the image, but the entire group paused and looked over their shoulders.

On the Big Top Parade and Circus Celebration weekend in July 2017, a group of former clowns took the Circus of Ghouls tour at the Circus World Museum Ring Barn with Baraboo Tours. The tour ran from 2016 to 2017 and was touted as being part paranormal, part illusion show and part haunted house. Afterward, each guest was given ghost hunting equipment to explore the building on their own. Five clowns stayed with the guide, who had an electromagnetic field (EMF) detector called a Ghost Meter Pro. Once a spirit attached itself to the Ghost Meter Pro, it could answer yes or no questions. Typically, on the tour, the group connected with the spirits of deceased circus performers or other circus workers. On that particular night, however, the spirit replied that it was not a previous circus worker. One clown, Annette Darragh, said to the group, "Well, my dad passed away recently, and I will know it is him if a dime appears." As the group processed this information, a dime fell out of the guide's flashlight and onto the floor. The clown scooped up the dime and said, "Thanks, Dad." After a moment of disbelief, another clown grabbed the flashlight and said, "I want a one-hundred-dollar bill!" Nothing appeared, but many more attempts were made that night.

12

Circus World Museum

550 Water Street, Baraboo, Wisconsin

Circus World Museum is a National Historic Landmark recognizing the Ringling Brothers Circus headquarters and winter grounds, as well as the influences of the Gollmar and Moeller families. A number of original buildings remain on the property, where circus animals were housed in the winter and the circus prepared for its next season. Visitors make their way through historical exhibits of circus-related memorabilia and enjoy a daily Big Top show presented by performers who are hired annually, many of whom stay on-site. In the late 1970s, a tiger trainer told museum staff of an experience she had in the middle of the night while sleeping in her truck on the grounds of Circus World Museum. She woke to a loud clap of thunder during a lightning storm and saw a scene from the early 1900s. A circus tent appeared outside her truck. Women in long dresses, big hats and parasols and men in suits walked around her to go into the tent. After another bolt of lightning, the scene was gone. She admitted that the whole thing sounded like a dream, but she swore she was wide awake.

Robert L. Parkinson Library and Resource Center

For a few years in the early 2000s, Circus World Museum employees wondered if the spirits from the notoriously haunted Old Baraboo Inn were making their way onto circus property. The Robert L. Parkinson

The Big Top tent at Circus World Museum. *Courtesy of Bill Johnsen.*

Library and Resource Center (RPLRC) is located two lots down from the Old Baraboo Inn, on Lynn Street, where the Miller-Bender Brewery once stood. The RPLRC preserves the nation's largest repository of circus artifacts and ephemera with a state-of-the-art security system and controls for temperature and humidity. The current executive director of Circus World Museum, Scott O'Donnell, was the operations director back then and repeatedly received calls in the middle of the night from the Baraboo Police Department telling him that the security alarm had been tripped in the building. The strange thing was that the alarm would consistently go off exactly seventeen minutes after the alarm at the Old Baraboo Inn was triggered. It got to the point that the Baraboo Police Department would call Scott and tell him to get ready whenever they responded to the security alarm at the Old Baraboo Inn. Scott would get out of bed and, in the dark of night, drive down to the RPLRC. He joined the police on the street, watching and waiting. Seventeen minutes later, like clockwork, the security alarm would trip in the RPLRC, and Scott would unlock the door and join the officers with flashlights to clear the building. They never found anything or figured out how the alarm was triggered so frequently or why it coordinated with the alarm system at the Old Baraboo Inn. The building was airtight to protect the circus collections and never had vermin running around that might have tripped the motion sensors.

Ring Barn: The Man Is Here

Circus World Museum's Ring Barn on Water Street has caused many people to scratch their heads at the unexplained occurrences inside. It was originally built with stalls for horses and constructed with a ring in the back, similar to the ring of a circus tent, where circus performers practiced performances in the off-season. Today, the Ring Barn is open to the public and full of iconic circus memorabilia, such as plaques, circus wagons, clown exhibits and photographs of circus performers.

In 2001, Shelley Mordini's first inclination that something wasn't right in the Ring Barn came when she brought Amy, a young woman with Down syndrome, to work as part of a program that brings meaningful opportunities to students with disabilities. Amy's job was to erase whiteboards that were being used to teach kids how to make clown faces, among other tasks at the museum. Shelley and Amy worked twice per week, and one day, as they got to work, Shelley opened the door to the Ring Barn and Amy stopped, refusing to enter. Amy used sign language to communicate because she could not vocalize well.

"No work. The man is here," she signed.

An external view of the Ring Barn at Circus World Museum. *Courtesy of Pam Thompson.*

They were the first people to enter the barn for the day, and no one else was around. Shelley, confused about what Amy was talking about, impatiently signed back, "We have to go to work."

Amy signed again, "No work. The man is here."

Frustrated, Shelley left Amy at the door to wipe off the clown faces herself. They continued with the job list at the other buildings, and Amy completed all other tasks without a problem. The next time they arrived at the door of the Ring Barn, Shelley signed to Amy, "Well, is the man here today?"

Amy signed no, looking a little confused, and went right in to work. The man appeared to Amy about once a month while working in the Ring Barn. After the first few times, Shelley tried again, unsuccessfully, to get Amy to go to work when the man was present. She always refused.

As to who the man was, no one knows for sure. Harold "Heavy" Burdick has been in charge of ground maintenance at Circus World Museum for forty years. He also believes a male spirit is attached to the Ring Barn, due to a number of experiences he had while cleaning the building in the early morning. For example, one morning while sweeping the Ring Barn, Heavy saw a shadowed apparition walk out of a wall and then through a door that led to the old tack room for horses. The dark apparition was only half there, with a defined head and misty body. It appeared to be an older man with an old-fashioned hat, big nose and defined chin. Heavy got the impression that the apparition was an old circus worker who was going to get some tack for the horses.

Another morning, Heavy unlocked the front door of the Ring Barn for a repairman who planned to arrive early. As he cleaned, he heard the door open and slam shut. Heavy yelled out to see if it was the repairman who entered. The man answered, "Yeah, I'm here!" Heavy finished cleaning and left, only to receive a call an hour later from the repairman apologizing that he couldn't make it. He thought back and realized that the voice was an older man's voice, and he wondered if it was the same male spirit he saw walk through the wall.

Heavy also had an early-morning encounter in the Ring Barn with a spirit that appeared to be female, and it came in the form of footprints on the floor. For a period of time, the roof leaked and left a large puddle near the ramp after a rain. Heavy arrived one morning with a mop and saw half of a footprint coming out of the puddle, then another a step away. The footprints were small and looked like a lady's shoe.

13

St. Mary's Ringling Hospital

103 Tenth Street

Ask any Baraboo resident which buildings in town are haunted, and most will mention the old hospital on the corner of Tenth and Oak Streets. The abandoned three-story building has been unoccupied for almost two decades. Residents who are old enough to remember the hospital in its heyday remember visiting for various reasons; some were born there, and others had relatives who died there. Today, most of the windows have all been broken out; it is full of mold and contains asbestos. Some neighbors describe hearing strange noises from the building, and others have even seen lights through the windows, though the electricity was cut off years ago. A few investors have shown interest in the property, but when they discover that it would cost $1.5 million to restore the building, they lose interest. The City of Baraboo has tried for years to secure enough money to help with the costs to demolish the building, but nothing has gone through. Some neighborhood residents wonder what will happen to the ghosts when the building is torn down, hoping that the ghosts don't take up residence in their homes.

These days, the building sometimes gives onlookers the heebie jeebies, but it wasn't always that way. It was originally the mansion of Alfred "Alf" T. Ringling and his first wife, Della (Andrews) Ringling. Alf T., one of the original five Ringling brothers, was a talented musician. Born in 1863, he was eleven years younger than his older brother Al., but as soon as he was old enough, he accompanied his brother in the early days by playing cornet, violin and several brass instruments. Later, when the Ringling Brothers

A modern street view of the former St. Mary's Ringling Hospital. *Courtesy of Pam Thompson.*

Circus officially took off, he managed press relations, regularly submitting news articles about the circus to the press. His knack for writing and tendency to exaggerate made him quite successful at advertising the circus.

Alf T. married Della, and they had two children. In 1899, Alf T. hired Fred Kees of Minneapolis to design a fourteen-room mansion for his family at this location. The home had a library, ballroom, dining room, fancy chandeliers and bathrooms lined with colorful Delft tiles. Della filed for divorced in 1913, and by 1916, Alf T. had moved to Oak Ridge (then known as Petersburg), New Jersey, remarried and built a twenty-eight-room mansion, where he died on October 29, 1919.

Della continued to live in the mansion on Tenth Street until her children were grown. In 1922, she began exploring her options to donate the mansion to be used as a boys' home, but her priest, Father Edward C. O'Reilly, and her doctor, Dr. Daniel Kelly, asked if she would consider donating the mansion for use as a hospital instead. At the time, the nearest hospital was fifty-five miles away in Madison, Wisconsin. Few people had the means to travel such a distance, so local doctors often treated sick or injured patients on house calls or as outpatients. Della accepted and started a new era of healthcare availability in Baraboo. Father Edward secured an order of nursing nuns, the sisters of St. Mary of St. Louis, Missouri, to administer and serve the hospital. It was the same order that opened St. Mary's Hospital in Madison a decade before.

With substantial donations from the community, renovations to the mansion began on August 14, 1922. Many of the beautiful rooms in the mansion became patient wards. An addition was built on the north side of the house for an operating room, laboratory, X-ray room and more patient rooms. The ballroom transformed into the nurses' station. The local Elks Club received the dining room chandelier, and the pipe organ went to St. Joseph Catholic Church. St. Mary's Ringling Hospital opened on November 2, 1922, with twenty-five available beds for patients. Until ambulances became available after World War II, anyone in need of medical care without the means to travel were brought to the hospital by a hearse from the local funeral parlor.

Most Baraboo residents who are old enough to remember the old hospital have fond memories of the care provided there and the nuns who served the community. Some residents remember playing in the courtyard as children while waiting for their fathers to hold up their new brother or sister in the hospital window. Others who grew up in the neighborhood remember the nuns being an integral part of the community, offering sugar cookies out of the kitchen door and playing baseball in the parking lot on summer evenings. Sister Mary Clement could reportedly hit a baseball to the top of the roof.

An external view of Alf T. Ringling's mansion in 1921, before it was donated for use as a hospital. *Courtesy of Circus World/Wisconsin Historical Society.*

Soon, the hospital served not only Baraboo residents but also residents of nearby towns. The appearance of the mansion changed substantially over the years, as the hospital required more renovations in 1936, then again in 1946, to accommodate the rising number of people in need of service. A two-floor addition was added to the front, replacing the porch, as well as a three-story addition in the back for more patient beds. The renovations allowed for a number of updates as well, and St. Mary's Ringling Hospital became the first hospital in Wisconsin to have piped-in oxygen.

In 1959, the State of Wisconsin Board of Health determined that St. Mary's Ringling Hospital could no longer adapt to the modern requirements of a healthcare facility. After the new St. Clare Hospital opened a few blocks away, the sisters began offering nursing home services in 1963 and changed the hospital's name to St. Mary's Ringling Manor. Again, in 1975, building code requirements caused the sisters to close St. Mary's Ringling Manor entirely and retire from active duty. The property became St. Mary's Ringling Convent and served as a northern retirement

The sisters from St. Mary's Ringling Hospital. *Courtesy of SSM Health, St. Clare Hospital.*

home for the sisters of St. Mary (the southern home being located in St. Louis, Missouri). At this time, the renovations necessary to convert the hospital back to a living space resulted in the demolition of the original mansion, as well as other outbuildings.

In 1998, the remaining sisters of St. Mary's left Baraboo and sold the property to a business owner who wanted to turn the building into apartments, but he died before that project was complete. The building has been vacant ever since.

Before the building fell into such a state of disrepair, Paranormal Investigators of Sauk County (PISC) staged a ghost hunt after arranging special permission to be in the building. They wanted to see if the rumors were true about the building being haunted. In July 2011, Tom Dyar, cofounder of the PISC, prepared for a three-day exploration of the building. Why three days? Tom says it takes time for a ghost to become comfortable enough for meaningful dialog. A person can see ghosts in less time, of course, but the ghosts are usually running away or the person is running from the ghosts. During their initial walkthrough, the team got many images of shadows and voice recordings on their equipment. Ghosts are known to drain batteries, so they set up a command post on the third floor with a generator on the roof. The cords ran down the elevator shaft to power their equipment.

Inside the hospital, a participating mother quickly lost track of her teenaged son in the maze of hallways, and he had their flashlight. There were still plaques on the walls, a few old beds and a holy water basin attached to the wall in the chapel. She peered into the ambulance bay on the main floor and shouted her son's name into the darkness. Hearing a low, garbled response, she entered the room and called again. The garbled response kept her inching into the room a few more times until her son came up from behind and yelled for her to stop. He shined the flashlight in front of her to show a flight of stairs leading to the basement.

Throughout the weekend, the team witnessed small shadows, like a raccoon had just run out of a closet, but there wasn't anything there. They heard murmuring voices and footsteps behind them as they worked their way through the broken glass in the hallways. At one point, they heard a cheerful, disconnected voice reverberating through the hallways, saying, "Well, how are you?" Apparitions of nurses showed up in photographs—one holding a clipboard and another appearing to be holding a baby. Their headdresses and crosses could be seen in the photographs. But like many photographs taken in dark rooms, the quality was poor and left more questions than answers.

The room behind the chapel appeared to have the most concentrated amount of activity. Tom preferred the use of voice recorders but also facilitated conversations with the ghosts using two mini Maglites. These small flashlights have a twisting mechanism on the bulb end to turn the light on and off. He twisted the two flashlights until the light was just barely turned off and set them on a table. The spirits were then able to turn the flashlights on to answer yes-or-no questions. The spirits turned on the purple flashlight for yes and the black flashlight for no. He preferred this method to a Ghost Meter Pro, an EMF (electromagnetic frequency) detector, because of the elimination of false hits due to electrical interference from wires and appliances. They asked the spirits why they were attached to the hospital. They wondered if the spirits were trapped or if they had died there. They discovered that most spirits were there because it was the last place they remembered, or they were at the hospital all the time when they were alive.

Near midnight, the mother returned to the old hospital to pick up her teenage son. She parked in the hospital parking lot, aiming her headlights into a door that had been propped open. Shadows moved around inside, and she heard tables being dragged across the floor. Her son did not come out. After fifteen minutes, she called him and asked when he would be coming outside. He informed her that everyone was upstairs on the third floor, not on the main level, doing an EVP (electronic voice phenomenon) session. They would be down shortly. Nervously, she rolled up the windows and locked her doors while she waited for her son to arrive.

At approximately 3:00 a.m. on the last night of exploration, the generator ran out of gas and abruptly died, leaving all of the ghost hunters in the dark on the third floor. Not one person had a working flashlight after so many hours of exploring in the dark. Putting their hands on the wall for guidance, they began walking through the labyrinth of hallways toward the first floor. A bright volleyball-sized orb came out of the ceiling at the end of a long hallway. It looked like a light on the ceiling, causing momentary confusion because the building did not have power. The lighted ball slowly floated down the hallway in a meandering pattern toward them, stopping for a moment at each door. The group felt like they were witnessing the spirit of a nurse checking on the patients. They stood in awe as it approached, closer and closer; then the orb transformed into a large mist and charged at them like a bear with ghost-like arms, apparently in an attempt to shoo them away. They wrapped it up for the night and hastily left the building.

14

Al. Ringling Mansion

623 Broadway Street

The mastermind behind the Ringling Brothers Circus, Al. Ringling, built a mansion on the north side of the downtown square. To say that strange things sometimes happen inside would be an understatement. Apparitions, orbs, shadows, disconnected voices and touches are common occurrences on all levels of the home. Mediums and psychics have said there are at least twenty to twenty-five spirits residing there. No one knows who all of the spirits are, but Al. Ringling and his wife, Lou, are among them. At eighteen thousand square feet, there certainly is enough room for all of them.

Al. Ringling was the oldest of eight children in the Ringling family. In his early years as a circus performer, Al. specialized in juggling, acrobatics and balancing acts. He could walk a tightrope from one building to another and successfully balance a seventy-pound wooden hand plow on his chin. He met snake charmer Eliza "Lou" Morris, and the two were married on December 19, 1883. As a talented seamstress, she would eventually be in charge of the wardrobe department for the circus.

When money began pouring in from the success of the Ringling Brothers Circus, Al. and Lou bought property on Broadway Street, near Baraboo's city center, and hired contractors Carl and George Isenberg to oversee the construction of a mansion. When completed in 1906, the building, which was made of Lake Superior sandstone, was the grandest and most exotic-looking house in Baraboo, suggestive of their fame and world travels. With four bedrooms, it was beautifully designed to include decorative walls and ceilings, maids' quarters and a ballroom in the basement.

An external view of the mansion built by Al. Ringling. *Courtesy of Pam Thompson.*

Al. and Lou lived in the house with their staff while managing the circus for the next decade. Not much was written about their relationship at the time, but at some point, their great partnership began to show some strain. After a number of miscarriages, Al. and Lou were unable to have children. At one point, Lou remarked that Al. was more fun before becoming wealthy. The two quarreled about a theater that Al. proposed building in Baraboo as his health began to deteriorate. Al. filed for divorce shortly before his death, but the couple reportedly reconciled their differences soon after. Al. Ringling passed away in the mansion on January 1, 1916, at the age of sixty-three, from Bright's disease, a form of kidney disease.

After Al.'s death, Lou had little interest in the mansion and purchased a house a few blocks away on the corners of Ash and Sixth Streets, where she lived until she died in 1941. Al.'s sister Ida Ringling North moved into the mansion with her family for a few years, but by 1927, the mansion stood empty. Two decades after being built, the mansion was slated to be torn down to save on taxes. At one point, a wrecking crew was reportedly in town to begin the demolition process, but negotiations continued, and the mansion was saved. In 1936, the Baraboo Elks Club bought the building at a generously discounted price ($6,000) from the Ringling North family and used it as their lodge for almost eighty years.

Lou Ringling as a snake charmer in the circus, 1889. *Courtesy of Circus World/Wisconsin Historical Society.*

One of the first things Joe Colossa learned about the mansion as he began to negotiate for its purchase was that it was haunted. Some Elks Club members claimed to have seen an apparition of a little girl in the basement and a woman on the stairs in a Victorian dress. They also asserted that a shot glass of whiskey that was left on a mantel had mysteriously emptied and flipped over while no one was looking. But Joe was unphased. His family had been involved with the circus for four generations. Joe was no stranger to circus spirits. He worked for fourteen years as a circus train master with the Ringling Brothers and Barnum & Bailey Circus, and a few of the circus train cars were thought to have been haunted. He had a vision for the old mansion of Al. Ringling, a man he'd been interested in since he was eight years old. Joe purchased the mansion with his wife, Carmen, and Don Horowitz.

Joe and his family became the first people to live in the mansion since the Ringling North family had moved out eighty years before. They initially moved into the maids' quarters so that work could begin on the rest of the house. His first ghost encounter soon followed. While reading in bed late in the evening, when the house was quiet, he felt a bump at the end of the bed, as if someone had just walked into it. It was not his imagination. He set down his book and spoke to the room because he heard somewhere that might help. He told the spirit that he would be staying at the mansion and that he planned to fix it up. He went on to insist that the spirits leave him alone in his own space, but that they were free to do as they pleased in the rest of the house. Since then, he hasn't had any problems. Not even after moving into an apartment they built in the attic, which was previously an area of high paranormal activity.

However, the rest of the house was a different story. At first, Joe and Carmen often thought someone else was in the house with them. They'd hear footsteps on the grand staircase after midnight, only to find an empty hallway when they got up to check. They would often catch something in their peripheral vision, but then they would see nothing when they looked straight on. One day, after returning from the store, Carmen saw an intruder in the house through a window on the veranda. The man was looking into a mirror in the side hallway. He was startled when she put the key in the door and took off around the stairs. After searching, they were unable to find anyone in the house. At some point, Carmen realized the man looked like a Ringling brother, and perhaps, the intruder was actually an apparition. She did not see the man well enough to identify him as Al. Ringling.

Al. and Lou Ringling on a circus lot, date and location unknown. *Courtesy of Circus World/ Wisconsin Historical Society.*

While conducting a tour of the mansion, Joe saw an apparition of Al. Ringling through the mirror on the wall. He was standing in the foyer with his signature mustache, and he wore a black suit with a high white collar. He then walked out the front doors, though the doors did not move. The apparition looked so real that someone asked if Joe had people working in the house in period clothing.

The original bedroom set that belonged to Lou Ringling was returned to the mansion, making Lou's bedroom one of the most authentic in the

An interior view of Lou Ringling's bedroom with her original bedroom set. *Courtesy of Pam Thompson.*

mansion. When Joe's daughter was four, he found her staring into Lou Ringling's bedroom, giggling and laughing. He asked her what she was laughing at, and she replied, "Lou! She is trying on dresses in front of the mirror, but she keeps turning around and making faces at me."

For surveillance around the house, Joe set up video cameras and motion lights, which turn on simultaneously when the motion of a person or something solid is detected in the room. After the cameras repeatedly turned on without the lights, Joe now believes that, for whatever reason, the movement of spirits can trigger only the video cameras but not the motion lights. He captured a video of an apparition of a little boy running across foyer and then into Al. Ringling's library.

These days, Joe hardly notices the activity in the house anymore, but that doesn't mean it isn't happening. He sometimes works in the basement until late evening and hears disconnected voices, people talking, music playing and doors opening and closing, but he rarely bothers to check it out. People who visit the house, not used to things happening without reason, often report a lot of activity.

A relative stayed at the mansion one night and woke to find a cute boy, around six years old, looking at her. He stood near the door of her bedroom. She got up, hoping to communicate with him, but he faded away as she approached. She noted that the boy was Black, and at one point, the Ringling's had a Black maid, so perhaps this child was hers.

A mason from Chicago was staying in one of the bedrooms and heard footsteps in the middle of the night, walking around the second-floor parlor, and someone tried his door handle.

Paranormal occurrences in the mansion are rarely scary, but some can be disconcerting at times. Witnesses report hearing disembodied name calling, and people even report hearing their own names being called. Blankets are sometimes pulled off of people in their beds, and other times, they feel the sensation of someone sitting or moving on the bed next to them.

Some witnesses report getting touched by unseen entities, such as shoulder taps or hair pulling. One actor at a *Titanic* reenactment dinner that was held at the mansion became so put out after getting her bottom grabbed while standing alone in a room that she had to go outside to get some air.

Today, the mansion offers one of the largest collections of Ringling brothers artifacts in the world. Joe has built a relationship with the Ringling family and has been able to acquire things that belonged to almost every brother. Joe also found Al. Ringling's original beer recipe hidden in the house, which is now available through the Al. Ringling Brewing Company on site. The mansion is open daily for tours, with haunted tours by request. They plan to offer guest rooms for overnight stays.

15

Al. Ringling Theatre

136 Fourth Avenue

The manager of the Al. Ringling Theatre keeps a ghost light on stage to appease the spirits who reside in the theater. A ghost light is a simple floor lamp placed in the middle of a stage at night. The last person to leave the theater turns it on, and the first person to enter the next day turns it off. This is a theater tradition that stretches back for centuries. It is thought that if the spirits are allowed space to perform after hours, then they won't disrupt the theater during live performances. The Al. Ringling Theatre has plenty of spirits. Ghost lights also have practical purposes, of course, such as lighting up an otherwise dark theater in order to provide safe passage for personnel. The original ghost lights were thought to be lit by gas, and the practice of leaving a light burning on stage may have prevented pressure from building up in the lines.

In his book *The Phantom Finger and Other Ghost Stories from the Al. Ringling Theatre*, M. Richard Tully describes a plethora of ghostly encounters inside the theater. Among them, Tully tells the legend of the woman in white, a transparent apparition often seen in the back of the theater wearing a white dress, searching for her baby who fell from the balcony and disappeared. Many witnesses in charge of the sound system have reported hearing a baby crying through the audio equipment during performances. Tully also addressed a rumor that the theater was built with hidden underground tunnels and passages that some boys allegedly ventured into and never returned from. No tunnels or passages have ever been found, and no one knows who the boys were, but tapping can still be heard on the pipes because

The ghost light on stage at the Al. Ringling Theatre. *Courtesy of the Al. Ringling Theatre.*

it is thought that the boys are eternally looking for a way out. Perhaps the most unusual story is that of the phantom finger. Tully links a number of unexplained touches, manipulated switches and strikes of wrong notes on instruments to a severed index finger that a man lost while unloading steel during the construction of the theater.

In 1912, Al. and Lou Ringling set out to build America's Prettiest Playhouse as a gift to Baraboo. The original opera house in Baraboo had burned down a decade before, and the city was in desperate need of a replacement. Al. saw this as an opportunity to leave a legacy in Baraboo. They purchased the Wisconsin House hotel, which dated to 1850, and had it torn down immediately. Al. hired Chicago firm C.W. and George L. Rapp to design the theater, which many people believe is based on Ange-Jacques Gabriel's opera house of the Palace of Versailles in Paris, France. The completed theater included whimsical murals on the ceilings, a replica of Luca Della Robbia's *Singing Gallery* figures in the main lobby, 874 seats on the main floor, 17 box seats and 11 dressing rooms.

At some point leading up to the construction of the theater, Al. and Lou began quarreling, and Al. filed for divorce in the spring of 1914. By August 1914, instead of proceeding with the divorce, the couple appeared to have reconciled, and Al. gave Lou $100,000, which was an amount equal to the cost of building the theater. Shortly after, Al.'s health began deteriorating, and no one was sure if he would live to see the theater complete. Fifty workmen assembled to build the theater as quickly and efficiently as possible. Construction of the theater began in March 1915 and was completed by November that same year.

The Al. Ringling Theatre opened on November 17, 1915, with the comic opera *Lady Luxury*. Al. sat in the center box seat with members of his family on opening night. His eyesight was failing, and Lou whispered in his ear most of the details that he was unable to see. Al. died a month and a half later in his mansion, on January 1, 1916. The surviving Ringling brothers offered the theater to the City of Baraboo in 1917, but the city declined the gift because of legal attachments. The Ringling family continued to own the theater until 1953, when it was sold to private owners. It was placed in the National Register of Historic Places in 1976. The theater is now owned by Al. Ringling Theatre Friends, a community-based nonprofit organization.

An external view of the Al. Ringling Theatre shortly after it was built in 1915. *Courtesy of Kandie Beckwith.*

Al. Ringling's ghost is thought to still occupy the center box seat (box 17). For years, witnesses have reported seeing a man resembling Al. Ringling—at least for an instant—waiting for a show to begin. After renovations in 2016, a set builder for the production of *Beauty and the Beast* became aware of Al.'s presence. He brought his three-year-old daughter to work with him, and at one point she wandered away. He found her looking out into the audience from the stage and waving with a huge smile on her face. Not seeing anyone in the theater, he asked who she was waving to. "The man!" she said, pointing toward the middle box seat. Troubled, he brought her over to play closer to him, but she still insisted that she saw a man. As they left the theater that day, the little girl saw a portrait of Al. Ringling hanging on the wall in the lobby and said, "That's the man I was waving to, Daddy!"

Few people who frequent the theater find the spirits spooky, but the spirits do catch people off guard sometimes. Stall doors in the bathroom have been known to repeatedly slam shut while the other stall is occupied. The apparition of a twelve-year-old girl with a poufy dress and blond hair in ringlets has been known to run along the stage and make the curtains move. She has also been known to interact with little girls during dance recitals, sometimes tricking them into going to places in the theater that they are not allowed to go to.

Kori Griffin, the 2016 stage manager for the Baraboo Theatre Guild (BTG) had a post-show discussion with the director, producer, lighting person and the stage manager. All of the cast and orchestra had gone home for the evening, and the theater was empty. They stood off to the side of the stage, in the wings, near the dressing rooms, when they heard the most beautiful violin music playing. It was very peaceful and came from the back of the theater, toward the exit. They didn't bother to see who was playing until they remembered that the orchestra did not have a violinist, so it couldn't have been anyone from the production. The moment they looked out into the audience, the music stopped playing, and they soon confirmed that the theater was empty.

While watching a movie in the theater as a young girl, Mary Schaefer saw the apparition of a preteen boy for the first time. He was sitting above the organ pipes with his pants rolled up to his knees and one leg dangling over the edge. He wore a white shirt with black suspenders and a hat. He showed up again when she was in high school, waiting to go on stage. He looked exactly the same as he sat watching the show on the black boxes. They looked at each other as she entered the stage, but when she got back from performing, he was gone. In 2015, she was hired as a concessionaire,

Above: A view of the interior of the Al. Ringling Theatre from the stage. *Courtesy of Bill Johnsen.*

Left: Some box seats in the Al. Ringling Theatre are known to have spirits attached to them. *Courtesy of Al. Ringling Theatre.*

and as she went to flip off the lights at the end of the night, she saw the boy again. She didn't recognize him immediately and instead apologized to him because she thought he was a performer. He walked toward her with his mouth moving, but she could not hear what he was saying. Only after he faded away did she realize that it was the boy she had seen twice before.

Mary also had a run-in with a notoriously territorial shadow spirit that is known to frequent the box seat on the far left of the theater. It is nearly six feet tall, slim and appears as a full-body 3-D shadow apparition. Mary was cleaning the box seat on her hands and knees and stood up after picking up popcorn. Suddenly, she saw the shadow man between her and the hallway. By then, she had worked at the theater for a considerable amount of time and had accepted that ghost encounters happened from time to time. In a stern voice, she told the shadow that if he wanted his space clean, she had to be able to do her job. The spirit apparently did not appreciate her tone, because moments later, she felt a hand enter her abdomen and squeeze. Her organs constricted uncomfortably for a couple of seconds before it subsided. She felt like he was telling her it was his space. She immediately gathered her supplies and left for the evening.

16

Charles Ringling House

201 Eighth Street

The Ringling mansion on Eighth Street, locally known as the Yellow House, had been in the Ringling family for over a century before Julie and her partner bought it in 2015. They were looking for an older home with historical significance where they could open a bed-and-breakfast. As a skeptic, Julie never put much thought into ghosts occupying the old mansion—at least, not until a few strange experiences caused her to wonder if there was, in fact, a ghost in the house. The mansion was designed by Ferry & Clas, a prestigious Milwaukee architectural firm, in the Georgian Revival style for Carl Edward "Charles" Ringling and his wife, Edith (née Conway). It was completed in 1901. Charles was the fifth son in the Ringling family and was mainly in charge of advertising and promoting the circus. He managed the group of employees who were responsible for plastering circus posters across the countryside prior to the show's arrival. Charles was the most musically talented of all of the brothers and designed his home with a music room on the first floor. The nearly two-acre property originally included a two-story carriage house and a smaller mother-in-law home facing Ninth Street.

Charles sold the mansion to his youngest brother, Henry Ringling, in 1911. Although Henry joined the circus in 1886, he didn't become a partner until his older brother Otto died in 1911, leaving his fifth of the circus to Henry. He then became the superintendent of the main entrance to the Big Top. The mansion was then passed on to his son Henry E. Ringling Sr. and his wife, Jean; then it was passed on to their daughter Salome "Sally" Juliar

An external view of the Charles Ringling home, now known as the Ringling House Bed and Breakfast. *Courtesy of Pam Thompson.*

Ringling Clayton-Jones. The Ringling family hosted many dinner parties and holiday celebrations there over the years that typically involved singing and playing music among the partygoers. The property was listed in the National Register of Historic Places in 1997 for its historical significance as the home of Charles Ringling during the growth and expansion of the Ringling Brothers Circus empire.

For a time, the male members of Henry's lineage succumbed to a number of misfortunes that resulted in early deaths. Henry Ringling, the largest of the seven brothers at six foot, three inches tall and over three hundred pounds, died at age forty-nine of heart disease. His son Henry Ellsworth Ringling II also died at the age of forty-nine in 1955. His grandson Henry Ringling III died in 1962 outside of Baraboo in a car accident at the age of twenty-three. His granddaughter Sally did not die as young as her male relatives, but she still endured many tragedies. Not only did her grandfather, father and brother die when she was young, but in 1961, her fiancé, German racing driver Wolfgang von Trips, died in a crash at the age of thirty-three, and then her husband, pilot William Clayton-Jones, died in a plane crash at the age of forty-two. She retired at the mansion after her mother died and remained there until 2005, when she died of a stroke at the age of sixty-eight.

The house remained empty for nearly a decade before her children put the mansion up for sale in 2013, giving Julie and her partner an opportunity to purchase the home.

Strangely, Julie's first experience occurred shortly after they moved in, while she was napping in an upstairs bedroom that was previously occupied by Sally, now referred to as room 1. Julie was awoken by the sensation of someone sitting on the bed. She assumed her cat had jumped up onto the bed, but when she opened her eyes, the cat was not in the room, and the doors were closed. This happened on three separate occasions, and every time, the cat was not there. At first, she thought that maybe she was dreaming—but not after the third time.

Shortly after opening the bed-and-breakfast, she was vacuuming in room 1 when the overhead light suddenly went out. At first, she thought maybe she had blown a fuse, but the vacuum was still running. Then she thought the lightbulb had burned out, but it was unlikely that all of the bulbs in the fixture would burn out at the same time. She looked over at the light switch and saw that it had been turned off. All she could think of was how strange it was because she was the only person in the house at the time and couldn't

An interior view of room 1 in the Ringling House Bed and Breakfast. *Courtesy of Tom Krueger Photography.*

imagine how that could have happened. At that point, she started to wonder if there was a ghost in the house that wanted to get her attention.

Whether it was actually the spirit of Sally in the house or another previous occupant of the house is impossible to know. Visitors who stay in the room alone have also claimed to experience the sensation of someone sitting on the bed in the night. An old friend of Sally's stopped over to tour the bed-and-breakfast and to see the remodeled house. As they arrived in the bedroom upstairs, the woman began telling a story about Sally, and a brand-new LED lightbulb blew out in the fixture overhead. Of course, it could have been a coincidence, but after Julie's previous experiences in the room, she told the woman that she thought maybe Sally might be trying to say hi. The friend responded, "Well, if anyone could do it, Sally could."

At one point, Julie downloaded a ghost messaging app on her phone in an attempt to communicate with the spirit in the house. These apps tend to make strange noises and utilize random algorithms to create words or phrases, seemingly from a spirit. She used the app a couple of times with her friends, but she never learned anything profound. Months later, close to midnight, as Julie was putting laundry into a hallway closet outside of room 1, she heard a noise that sounded like a train whistle blowing on railroad tracks. She thought that was unusual because the mansion was too far from the tracks to hear the train from inside the house. She walked around and stood next to a couple of windows before realizing that the noise was coming from the phone in her pocket. The ghost app had somehow turned itself on and was generating words. Shaken, Julie put the phone back in her pocket. She was too freaked out to look at the message.

17

THE UNTIMELY DEATH OF ALBERTA GOLLMAR

BARABOO

The Shaker grandfather clock in the lobby of the Baraboo Public Library has a secret: it witnessed a murder in the kitchen of a house owned by Alberta Gollmar. The clock was later donated to the library by the estate of Alberta Gollmar in 1940, shortly after her untimely death. The clock was built by the Colonial Manufacturing Company in Zeeland, Michigan.

Alberta Gollmar was the wife of Charles Gollmar, one of the five brothers who started the Gollmar Brothers Circus in Baraboo. The Gollmar brothers were first cousins to the Ringling brothers—their mothers were sisters. The other nine children of Gottlieb and Mary Gollmar were not involved in the circus. The Gollmar Brothers Greatest of American Shows ran from 1891 to 1916, and along with the Ringling brothers, the Gollmar brothers wintered in Baraboo.

Alberta Gollmar (née Will) was Canadian and married Charles in 1899, when he was the manager of the circus. During Charles's tenure as the manager, the circus grew from a horse-and-wagon show to a thirty–train car show. Alberta traveled with her husband on the circus train and experienced all the thrills and hardships of the road for seventeen years. In 1918, they retired in Baraboo and bought a Sears and Roebuck home from the *Modern Homes* catalog and built it on a lot near downtown. The lot had been filled with soil that was removed during the construction of the Al. Ringling Theatre. They maintained a modest home together until Charles died of a heart attack in 1929. Charles and Alberta had made a

This Shaker grandfather clock, once owned by Alberta Gollmar, is now at the Baraboo Public Library. *Authors' collection.*

practice of feeding and housing former Gollmar Circus employees who were down on their luck. They eventually constructed an apartment in the basement to host these guests. After Charles passed, Alberta continued this practice but would often leave a pair of Charles's galoshes by the front door to suggest to strangers that a man was still in the home. She was often described as having scores of friends, a big heart and was always willing to help others.

In September 1938, Alberta rented the basement apartment to Richard Davidson, a former circus employee, and she arranged odd jobs for him to help him get back on his feet. For reasons unknown, Davidson attacked Alberta with a knife in the kitchen on September 21, 1938, as she made Rocky Mountain tea before retiring for the evening. Davidson stabbed her fifteen times, killing her. He then walked through the house to the bathroom, leaving a bloody trail; washed his hands and the knife; and then stole Alberta's money and jewelry. He left Baraboo by train and traveled to Milwaukee. Alberta's body was discovered the next day, and a manhunt followed to find her killer. The local police tracked Davidson to a boardinghouse in Milwaukee and set up a trap. When he returned to his room late on September 24, 1938, he tried to escape, but the police shot him through the door, piercing his lung and heart. He died at the scene. Police found Alberta Gollmar's purse and jewelry in Davidson's possession.

Two separate families who have since lived in Alberta's home had the same reaction on first entering the house: an overwhelming feeling of being welcomed. The home was designed to host large gatherings and to allow people to easily flow from room to room. It has hardwood floors, a fireplace and a large front porch. Very few renovations have taken place in the home, and the kitchen cabinets remain original to the home.

The kitchen still seems to be an area of unanswered questions by homeowners. When a previous owner, Kelly Dwyer, moved into the house with her family, it was completely empty. After a few weeks, the couple noticed that one of the kitchen drawers constantly got stuck while being opened. Kelly and her husband pulled hard on the drawer and discovered a set of old knives lodged in the back of the drawer. They knew that none of the knives was the murder weapon but noted that the knives looked to be from around the time the murder happened, and perhaps, they were part of the set. Then, on a January night, as Kelly cleaned the kitchen, she heard Christmas carolers outside the back door. They sang so loudly at the back door that she thought her friends were playing a joke on her, especially since it was January. She stepped outside, but no one was there. She looked around for a long time, then went back inside, only to hear the carolers again as soon as she got back to the dishes. She rushed back outside to silence, then went back inside and opened windows. She could not find the source of the singing and eventually chalked it up to her imagination but never knew for sure.

PART III

PRE-BARABOO

18
Early Inhabitants

People have lived along the Baraboo River, in the area we now call Baraboo, for centuries. The origins of the following experiences appear to predate the arrival of White settlers to the area or coincide with it. Historically, the Ho-Chunk were the most prominent Native peoples throughout the area. In their book *A Lake Where Spirits Live*, Kenneth Lange and Ralph Tuttle estimate that Natives have been living in the Baraboo area for four hundred generations (twenty-five years per generation). Archaeologists discovered one of the oldest known inhabited sites in the Midwest at Raddatz Rockshelter, just twelve miles from Baraboo, near the sandstone arch at Natural Bridge State Park. Paleoamericans used the site eleven thousand years ago, when the Wisconsin glacier was melting. It was added to the National Register of Historic Places in 1978.

So, it should be no surprise that when White people began arriving along the banks of the Baraboo River, they found an established Ho-Chunk village with a council house and cornfields. The shallow water in the river provided easy access to the other side and a place to harvest fish. There were also nearly one hundred earthen mounds, predating the village. Archaeologists believe that a group of people known as Effigy Moundbuilders formed the mounds during the late Woodland period, approximately one to two thousand years ago. The mounds vary in shape, from conical or linear to true effigies of local animals. Native stories suggest the mounds were used for ceremonial purposes and are sacred sites. Many were also used as burial sites. Few mounds remain today, as most were leveled by White settlers to

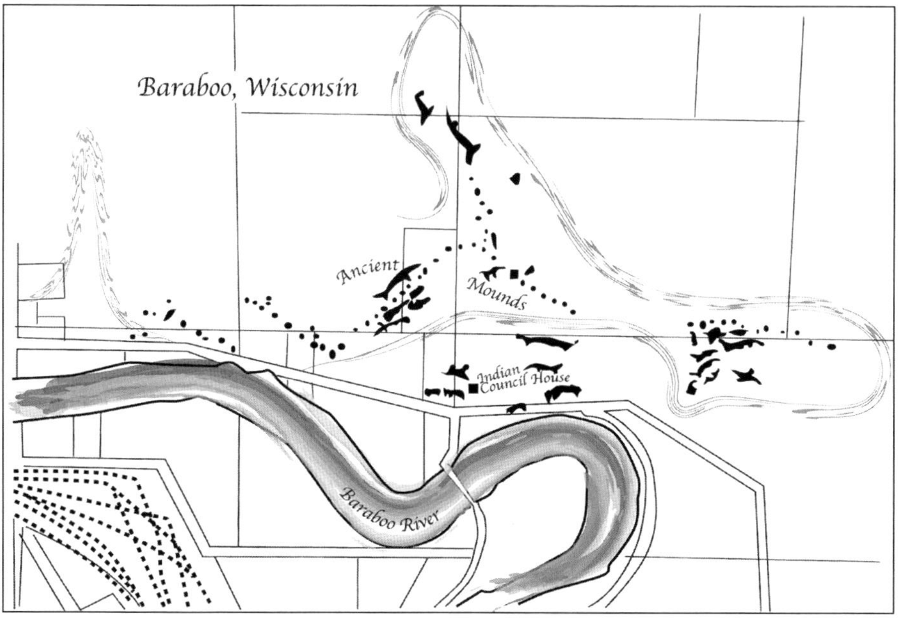

A map of the mounds that once lined the hillside at the corner of Water Street and Effinger Road. *Courtesy of Kyle Martin.*

construct roads, buildings and fields. Mound and Council Streets, near the Baraboo River, were named after these historical features.

The former existence of these ancient mounds in Baraboo neighborhoods has been sensationalized over the years. There are no ghost stories associated with effigy mounds. Any apparent supernatural experience within the proximity of a mound appears to be coincidental and cannot be substantiated whatsoever. They remain sacred sites for the Ho-Chunk people, and their destruction is extremely unfortunate.

19
SPIRIT PADDLER
DEVIL'S LAKE STATE PARK

Sometimes, in the early morning or late evening, when the water is calm and the air is misty with fog, visitors at Devil's Lake State Park claim to see the apparition of a Native paddling a wooden canoe on the lake. The apparition, which often appears to be transparent, is a male and dressed in traditional clothing. It disappears as quickly as it appears.

Who this spirit paddler may be is unknown. Natives inhabited Devil's Lake for centuries, and the area is still considered a sacred place. Several effigy mounds line the north and south shores—a lynx, a bear and a bird. Early White settlers noted a fishing camp at the north shore of the lake. A group of Ho-Chunk also camped at the south shore in the winter until at least 1900.

A view of Devil's Lake from the bluffs at Devil's Lake State Park. *Courtesy of the Baraboo Chamber of Commerce.*

Few people would likely be alarmed at the idea of a Native spirit paddling on the lake, even if they were lucky enough to witness it. Devil's Lake has drawn visitors for centuries, and most admit that there is an uncanny spiritual appeal. The Ho-Chunk name for the lake translates to mean "sacred" or "spirit lake." The area is part of the Baraboo Range, an ancient mountain range that geologists believe formed 1.6 billion years ago. The quartzite bluffs surrounding the lake are known to be some of the most ancient rock outcrops in North America. The lake itself didn't form until the Wisconsin Glacier made its way to Baraboo fifteen thousand years ago. It built up sediment, forming terminal moraines that dammed up the valley on two sides and rerouted a river that is thought to have previously flowed through the area. It is Wisconsin's largest and most visited state park, and it is in the National Register of Historic Places.

20

Ghost Wolves

Baraboo River

An eerie remembrance of the past has been observed on full moons or mostly full moons, when witnesses describe seeing swirling apparitions flowing down the Baraboo River, accompanied by the sound of howling wolves. The howling starts slowly at first, with just a lone wolf, then builds in number and intensity as if coming from an entire pack. The Ho-Chunk people highly respected wolves and recognized a Wolf Clan within their social organization, which was in charge of matters relating to health and safety. Oral traditions within the tribe, collected by the Milwaukee

A view of the Baraboo River as it winds through town. *Courtesy of Bill Johnsen.*

Public Museum from J. Owen Dorsey's article on Winnebago folklore notes in the *Journal of American Folklore* (1889), suggest that the (mythical) ancestors of the Wolf Clan were actually wolves.

Europeans began wolf elimination programs shortly after their arrival. The State of Wisconsin placed a bounty on wolves in 1865 that lasted for ninety-two years and resulted in the extirpation of wolves in the state by 1960, despite listing wolves as a protected species three years before.

It is said that the occurrence of ghost wolves often begins near the Baraboo Riverwalk at Mary Rountree Evans Park, and the swirling apparition ends at the footbridge that crosses the river at Circus World Museum. This phenomenon was reported by a number of people from all walks of life, many of whom knew the difference between howling wolves and yapping coyotes. It was also reported well before occasional wolf sightings were reported in Sauk County, as the population continues to rebound. Many witnesses believe that this phenomenon occurs because the souls of the wolves remain in the Baraboo River.

21
Spirit Warriors
Baraboo Bluffs

Some observers around Baraboo claim to have seen Native spirits traveling the bluffs and waterways of the Baraboo Area. Witnesses report shadows in the forests or full apparitions in traditional Native clothing. Sometimes, these spirits show up dancing around bonfires; other times, they appear to be fighting. Almost always, they are described as male warriors. The sight is often accompanied by the sound of shouts, screeches, whoops and the clashing of weapons. It is believed that these warriors are ancestors of the Ho-Chunk people, who have lived in the Baraboo area for thousands of years.

French explorers, the first White people to encounter Ho-Chunk warriors (probably near Green Bay in 1634), described them as powerful, well-built, skilled and fearless in the face of danger. Don Atkinson discussed Ho-chunk warriors at length in his book *Baraboo: A Selected History*, pulling much of his information from Paul Radin's comprehensive survey of the tribe in 1908. War was an important element in the Ho-Chunk culture, and being a warrior brought prestige, recognition and social standing within the tribe.

Over the centuries, many battles were fought between the Ho-Chunk people and the surrounding tribes. The Ho-Chunk were the only Siouan-speaking tribe in Wisconsin; all of the others were Central Algonquian tribes who had different languages, religions and social structures. Many other battles were fought with the new tribes arriving from the east, and then, later, with the American government or White prospectors who were too eager to wait for the legal transfer of land. Even after treaties were signed

Some claim to see spirit warriors in the wooded areas around the Baraboo Bluffs. *Courtesy of Pam Thompson.*

with the United States, the Ho-Chunk people successfully resisted numerous attempts by the government to remove the tribe from Wisconsin.

The only intact battle site in the Midwest from the American Indian Wars is located just fifteen miles from Baraboo. On July 21, 1832, Black Hawk led sixty warriors (mostly from the Sac, Fox and Kickapoo tribes) against seven hundred U.S. troops in what is now known as the Battle of Wisconsin Heights. Most Ho-Chunk avoided the war because they had just signed a treaty. The rest of the tribe took part on both sides; a few prepared to fight with Black Hawk, and others served as guides for the U.S. forces who followed Black Hawk and his people for over a week. There is evidence that the guides may have attempted to lead the militia through impassable swamps and tangled vegetation to slow their progress in catching Black Hawk and his people. Inevitably, when the militia caught up, Black Hawk was vastly outnumbered and lost over half of his warriors during the battle, but he saved nearly seven hundred of his people, as his strategy gave them time to escape down and across the Wisconsin River. The Wisconsin Heights Battlefield was listed in the National Register of Historic places in 2002.

Sightings of the spirit warriors have been reported throughout the Baraboo Bluff from Wisconsin Dells to Wisconsin Heights—possibly farther. Dennis

Boyer wrote of a similar phenomenon in 1996 in his book *Driftless Spirits: Ghosts of Southwest Wisconsin*, which he called the Rocky Arbor Battle Ghosts. The story outlines the legend of Red Horn as told from the perspective of a woman with whom the author had had a conversation. Warriors died in battle, and their spirits are thought to still travel the hillsides. Some say they are eternally locked in combat; others suggest that they are playfully fighting to refine their skills. The interpretation of spirit behavior may depend on one's cultural background. The spirits are rumored to still influence and protect the tribe.

Like all ghosts, spirit warriors are only seen when they want to be. Stand Rock, a natural amphitheater in Wisconsin Dells, was a place where Natives performed traditional dances for tourists from the 1920s until the 1990s. One time, a young girl watched as a Ho-Chunk dancer performed the closing ritual on the bluff above the amphitheater. Afterward, during the meet-and-greet, the young girl asked the dancer where the other performers were because she wanted to meet them. Confused, the adults told her the man danced alone, but the girl insisted that she saw a line of Natives step forward to stand with him at the end of the dance to close the ceremony. Small children are often able to see spirits that adults cannot.

PART IV

Private Residences

22
Residential Homes in Baraboo

With so many hauntings around town, it can only be expected that many of the houses in the Baraboo area have more than their fair share of strange occurrences. The first houses in Baraboo were simple log cabins built near the Baraboo River beginning in 1839. Early settlers took advantage of the river's forty-foot drop to power mills for sawing lumber, milling grains, shaping furniture and spinning wool. With the arrival of the railroad, more sophisticated styles of homes developed, as the building materials became more available, especially in affluent areas of town. Today, downtown Baraboo delights with a multitude of architectural styles from the latter half of the 1800s to the 1920s. A number of homes have a third-story ballroom, which was a common feature of the time that was used to entertain friends. Many of the historic homes are still single-family dwellings, but a number have also been turned into apartments or businesses. Each block away from the downtown square typically has more modern homes, as the decades of development marched out from the city center.

Hauntings are stereotypically associated with the large historic homes of Baraboo, but evidence shows that any house can have a spirit attached to it, whether it is old or new, and house style has little to do with it. Discovering a spirit in a house may be a scary experience for some, but most Baraboo residents take it in stride. Only one known incident of a poltergeist-type haunting, roughly in 2010, caused a family to back out of a rental agreement. After moving into a house on Mound Street, the family witnessed a shadowed apparition, electronics turning on by themselves and doors opening on their own. A young girl woke in the middle of the night numerous times with scratches on her skin in places that she could not have reached herself. Eventually, after finding themselves huddled together in a bedroom to sleep at night, the family moved out of the house.

The following stories have been gathered from Baraboo residents who witnessed hauntings. The streets on which the houses are located have been identified, but in many cases, house numbers and personal identifying information of the owners have been omitted to avoid unwanted attention to the property by curious onlookers.

23

The Lady of the House

Eighth Street

The Ruland* family woke in the morning to find all of the lights on in the house and the dining room table set for a dinner party of ten. Each place setting was professionally set with plates, silverware and wine glasses. Four-year-old Dana remembered that even the milk was on the table. The Rulands moved into the home on Eighth Street in 1969 with three young children. Four more children would soon follow. The house, like many historic homes in Baraboo, had chandeliers, pocket doors, a fireplace, an open staircase, a second set of stairs to the maids' quarters, a beautiful garden and a sizable attic. It also had a varied history of ownership. The house, almost in a state of disrepair from years of neglect, would be refurbished by the patriarch of the household in the decades to come.

When they woke to the lights on and table set, no one had a reasonable explanation for how it got that way—that is, no one except for seven-year-old Molly. She not only knew how it happened, but it appeared as if she was responsible for it. An apparition of a woman came to her in the middle of the night while she slept and beckoned for her to follow. The woman glowed slightly but was solid. She had white hair pulled up into a bun and a long flowing dress, which was also white. Molly and the woman walked all over the house, turning on the lights in each room along the way. They even went to the attic and basement, places where Molly typically refused to go alone during the day because she was afraid. The woman never spoke. She'd walk ahead of Molly and then turn around from time to time, coaxing her along with a motion of her hand. No one else woke up while Molly roamed around at night. The plaster walls in the large house muffled the sounds from the other floors in the house.

The apparition of the woman showed up so often that the kids began referring to her as the "Lady of the House." Molly was not afraid. It was the Lady of the House who coached her on the proper way to set a table, and she worked hard to get it right. After Molly and the Lady of the House finished with their business, Molly went back to bed. Her father woke a number of times, alarmed, when he heard her climbing the stairs, but she could never figure out why he looked so concerned.

Then the mother woke in the middle of the night to find an apparition of an old man in her bedroom. He wore bib overalls and had white hair. Similar to the Lady of the House, the apparition glowed slightly but looked solid. He walked through the bedroom to the southwest wall and disappeared. From that point on, the mother kept a broom at her bedside and played it off to the children as protection from the bats that frequently found their way into the house during the numerous remodeling jobs.

Molly's younger sister Dana was almost twelve years old before she witnessed anything in the house herself. Her first encounter was with a softball-sized orb in the hallway outside her bedroom door. She saw it as she lay in bed, trying to fall asleep. The orb was somewhat see-through, but it had a distinct, fuzzy edge. Confused at first, Dana studied the ball of light, which appeared near the metal light fixture in the hall, but it had a different glow than the hall light. It stayed visible for nearly fifteen minutes. From then on, orbs appeared under the doorframe to the bedroom that she shared with her younger sister Tina. Dana and Tina often watched the ghostly white ball shrink and expand or move in and out of the walk-in closet. Sometimes it disappeared, only to rematerialize again in the same spot.

Dana tried to discredit it, thinking maybe it was a streetlight shining through leaves outside and reflecting off of the mirror in the room. But the orb was a perfect circle, and it never formed according to the leaves blowing. Young Tina often watched the orb from her bed in the dark and pleaded with Dana to turn on the overhead light, but the light switch was next to the door, and Dana wasn't brave enough to venture the long walk across the room to turn it on.

The strange activity was not limited to the girls in the house. All four sisters woke one night to a whoomphing sound coming from somewhere in the house. Every few seconds, they heard it again. Two of the girls got up, clinging to each other, and walked into the hall. On the far wall in the room shared by their brothers, a radiator glowed a ghostly orange, intensifying in

An open staircase in a historic home in Baraboo. *Courtesy of Pam Thompson.*

color with each *whoomph*. The old radiator had been turned off for months because it was summertime. The noise also woke their oldest brother, who slept in a bed next to the radiator. He reached his hand out toward the orange glow and touched the radiator, but it was stone cold. The whoomphing sound stopped after he touched it.

The Lady of the House would also visit the youngest boy when he was around four years old. Similar to Molly's experience, the Lady of the House went to him multiple times in the middle of the night and beckoned him to follow. Only, she didn't appear to like him. She'd lead him to the top of the open staircase and encourage him to roll down. He considered doing it every time, then hesitated as he came to the realization of what he was about to do. He would have been severely injured, if not from the stairs, then by the bay of windows at the bottom of the stairs.

When Molly was a teenager, she stayed home for a weekend while the rest of the family went to visit their grandparents. She invited a neighbor friend to stay the night. In the middle of the night, Molly awoke to find her friend sitting straight up in bed, with the sound of something banging and rolling around in the attic. It sounded like someone was throwing a bowling ball around, and they had no desire to investigate.

The girls ran downstairs to use the house phone in the kitchen to call her friend's older brother and sister, and they asked them to come over because they were afraid of something that was in the house. By the time the siblings had arrived, the two girls were in the kitchen holding baseball bats, and the noise had followed them to the lower level of the house. The four teenagers stood in the kitchen, listening to the terrible banging and rolling for a few minutes before the sound exited out the southeast corner of the house, and all was silent.

After a couple of decades, the family moved out. The older kids never felt threatened by the presence in the house, but the youngest girl and boy in the family said they would never ever go back into that house again.

24

THE PHANTOM RADIO

NINTH STREET

Very few things are more maddening than being kept awake by annoying sounds. This is what happened to thirty-year-old Peggy Miller* when she rented a small house with her mother on Ninth Street in 1992. Everything was going smoothly until one spring night when Peggy woke to the muffled sound of a crazed radio announcer coming from her mother's bedroom—or so she thought. The radio announcer spoke excitedly, but she couldn't make out any of the words. Peggy thought that maybe her mother had bumped the clock radio next to her bed. She lay listening to this noise through the wall for quite some time, thinking, "Come on, Mom, turn it off."

Eventually, Peggy grew concerned that something might be wrong. She jumped out of bed and ran down the hall, the radio announcer's voice becoming louder and jabbering the whole time. She grabbed ahold of the doorknob to her mother's room, whipped open the door and—silence. The radio noise stopped the moment she opened the door. The room was dark. Her mother was sound asleep.

Unnerved, Peggy went back to bed. The next day, she asked her mother if she had heard anything during the night, but her mother had not. There were only two radios in the house: her mother's clock radio and her own. The noise obviously did not come from her own radio, since the announcer sounded muffled, and the closest house was at least thirty feet away.

Peggy shrugged off the experience until she awoke again in the middle of the night to the muffled sounds of opera music. It was beautiful music with a female singer, but it went on and on. She was unable to fall back to sleep. Annoyed, she got out of bed and walked around the room, putting her ear against all of the walls, the floor and the doors. The singing appeared to be coming from the built-in cabinet next to her bed, where she kept her clock radio, only her radio was off. She unplugged it to make sure. Baffled, she got back in bed and eventually managed to fall back to sleep, but she was exhausted the next day.

The sounds of the phantom radio continued on and off over a period of months. Peggy quickly grew tired of the phenomenon. One night, she woke when the radio announcer shouted: "Jim Kelley, dead at the age of forty-two!"

This time, the announcer's voice was loud and clear. It was just that one sentence and then silence. But of course, she couldn't fall back to sleep after that. Who the hell was Jim Kelley? And had he just died? Peggy actually knew of a couple local men named Jim Kelley, but neither one of them were around the age of forty-two at the time, and neither had died at that age.

Another night, Peggy woke to the sound of the same three descending notes of a musical instrument, like a recorder repeating over and over again—all night long. She dozed off occasionally but always woke to the same repetitive musical notes. Peggy grew angrier as the night went on.

Furious and exhausted, the next evening before bed, she sat on the edge of her bed and spoke to the room in a firm voice, "Alright, no crazed radio announcers, no opera singers, no three notes over and over again. That's it! I am done, and I do not want to hear anymore from you!" That night, Peggy slept straight through until early morning. Just before her alarm was set to go off, she was awakened by a *thbbbbbtf* (raspberry) next to her ear. She thought it was the spirits' way of saying, "We didn't wake you up all night, but the morning is fair game." That was the last time Peggy was ever woken by the phantom radio, and she lived in the house for another ten years.

25
The Chimney Room
Lynn Avenue

From the moment Lisa Young* toured the four-bedroom home on Lynn Avenue, she had a good feeling. The two-story house was built in the 1880s. It had character and a colorful history, albeit unusual. They were told that the scar on the chimney was from a time when the house had caught fire after being struck by lightning. They also heard rumors that it had once been a funeral home. But not even the large, steel, morgue-like slabs in the sandstone wall of the basement swayed her. In 1998, she and her husband purchased the home and moved in.

The house had a gorgeous gold-and-crystal chandelier that hung over the dining room table. It had been moved into the house from the Old Baraboo Inn, the most notoriously haunted bar in Baraboo. It was striking, but on closer inspection, the chandelier was more barbaric than beautiful, with half-human and gargoyle monsters etched into the gold. The owner of the Old Baraboo Inn offered to buy the chandelier back, but it was so thoroughly lodged in a beam that they decided to leave it in the house.

By chance, Lisa's husband ran into a woman who grew up in the house, and she still had some extra crystals for the chandelier. He invited her over, thinking that maybe she would like to bring the crystals over and to see the house since it was her childhood home. But the woman declined, stating that she would never set foot in that house again. The woman did not provide an explanation, and it was very clear that the conversation was over. Her strong reaction took the couple by surprise.

In 2001, Lisa began preparing a bedroom for the arrival of her daughter. Ultimately, she selected the upstairs room with the chimney lining one wall because the cats would not go into the room. The only problem was that the room was always cold and drafty. They did everything they could to bring more heat into the room, but nothing worked. In hindsight, the couple should have thought more about why the cats would not go into the room and why it was so cold. One day, Lisa was cleaning upstairs while her daughter, then three years old, played with a wooden peg puzzle in her bedroom. From two rooms over, she heard her daughter babbling in a way that was different than her normal babble. It was as if her daughter was talking to someone. Lisa looked in on her daughter and saw that she had taken out all of the puzzle pieces and lined them up across from her on the floor. Her daughter then pointed at a piece, picked it up and put it in the correct place, as if someone was coaching her. This was not something her daughter could do on her own at the time.

Lisa continued to watch her daughter put the whole puzzle together. Both she and her husband were educators, and nothing about the incident made sense. For starters, her daughter didn't have the puzzle pieces in a logical place. Most kids just dump the pieces next to them or in their lap. Her daughter deliberately lined up the puzzle pieces across from her as if they were displayed for someone else. She then pointed to each piece and waited, not looking at the pieces or the puzzle, but at someone across from her whom Lisa could not see. Lisa went in and sat down next to her daughter and tried to interact with her. It appeared as if her daughter was watching someone leave the room, paying no attention to her mom at all.

This type of behavior happened several times throughout the year, especially in the evening. There would be subtle differences each time, but Lisa always noted the behavior because their daughter babbled differently, as if she were speaking to someone. She'd ask questions, wait for answers and then respond herself as if she was having a conversation.

When her daughter transitioned from a crib to a normal bed, Lisa noticed that, sometimes, the blankets would, at some point, get pulled tight and tucked between the mattress and box spring—too tight. And it made Lisa uneasy because her daughter looked uncomfortable. This was a little girl who always kicked off her blankets and pajamas. She asked her husband if he was tucking in the blankets, and he said no.

Through the years, Lisa's daughter had an unusual attachment to the room upstairs, even though she set up a play area in the living room and a whole playroom on the first floor. Her daughter would play in the drafty room alone and often refused to leave it. When her daughter got older, Lisa asked her about the puzzle pieces and conversations in the bedroom. Her daughter said there was a little girl in her room who had long, stringy blond hair and wore pink-and-white striped overalls. Her daughter said the little girl was a bit older than her but noted that even though she was growing up, the little girl never aged. She said the little girl would often sit in the rocking chair, and her feet couldn't touch the ground. Her daughter was not afraid of the girl.

Lisa also asked her daughter if she remembered getting tucked in by the little girl. Her daughter didn't remember that specifically but indicated that the little girl's essence or some sort of power and strength hovered above the blankets at night. She felt like the little girl wasn't in her bed at night but was a bit above it.

Lisa's daughter wasn't the only one to have an unexplained experience in the house. One night, her husband came home and opened the cabinet door to a full-sized, built-in pantry in the kitchen. As he stood, looking at the food on the shelves, he saw a pair of women's feet and the hem of a white nightgown under the opened cabinet door. Whoever it was put pressure on the cabinet door. He let the door swing closed, but no one was there. Thinking it was his wife playing a trick on him, he ran upstairs, flipped on the lights and threw back the blankets of their bed. She was half asleep and wearing blue sweatpants. She obviously hadn't been downstairs.

The chimney was struck by lightning two more times while they lived in the house, but it never caused another fire. They installed more support, a deflector and a lightning rod, trying to avoid further damage to the house. The third time the chimney was struck, Lisa asked a power and light worker what else could be done to prevent it from happening again. He looked at her and said, "I would move."

Lisa and her family lived in the house until her daughter was twelve years old. The new owner contacted Lisa shortly after purchasing the property to specifically ask about the chimney room. Her boyfriend had been trying to sleep in that room because they worked opposite shifts, but he said the room made him feel uneasy.

26
THE WANDERING SPIRIT
EAST AND FIFTH STREETS

Over the decades, witnesses from multiple homes on East and Fifth Streets have reported seeing a three-foot-tall spirit; sometimes, it appears as a shadow, other times as a small boy. It is unknown if each story is about the same spirit, but their similarities and proximity indicate that perhaps it is.

Multiple owners of the same house on East Street, which was built in the 1880s, had children who witnessed shadows and apparitions. In 1969, five-year-old Tom Dyar lived in the house with his father, who began a project to remodel parts of the foyer. Whether or not that stirred up the spirit living in the house, one can only speculate. Tom first became aware of the spirit while lying in bed one night when he saw glowing red eyes in the bedroom closet. Whatever it was made noises and growled at him. He thought it was a demon.

Typically, the spirit only showed itself when Tom was alone, but he was not the only person the demon pursued. The only time Tom saw the demon outside of the closet was one evening when it followed Tom's grandfather down the hallway as he headed for the bathroom. It appeared as a red shadow on the wall, about three feet high, with what looked like fox ears on top of its head. Tom grabbed his toy dart gun and shot at it, hoping to protect his grandfather from the creature. The shadow quickly vanished. The commotion alerted Tom's father to the fact that he was out of bed and not asleep. Tom tried to explain that he saw a demon shadow, but his father accused him of making up stories and sent him to bed.

The marker for two streets where a small spirit is thought to roam between houses. *Authors' collection.*

Tom became determined. He had learned something that night about how to scare away the demon shadow. So, the next time Tom saw red eyes and heard the growling in his closet, he attacked. He jumped out of bed and sprinted toward the closet, but he lost consciousness right before reaching it. He woke up the next morning on the floor. The shadow never bothered him again.

Tom's dad sold the home to a new family a few years later. In 1975, a ten-year-old girl saw an apparition of a young boy floating above the stairs while she was falling asleep on a couch in the basement. The boy wore period clothing: knickers, a shirt with a collar, a small cap and leather shoes. He was transparent. She was not afraid of the boy and recalled thinking, "Oh, that's a little boy. He must live here." Then, as they continued to look at each other, she finally said, "Hello?" The boy disappeared, and she never saw him again.

On Fifth Street, not far from the East Street home, a woman also reported seeing a three-foot-tall shadow in 1995. One night, she woke from a sound sleep in her second-story apartment and felt like her whole body was pinned to the bed by a heavy weight. Only her eyes could move. A short, thin shadow stood at the bottom of the bed. It stared at her, motionless. The body was solid, its silhouette clearly outlined in front of the light shining on the wall from the street. Its head was an odd shape, bigger on the top and thinner toward the bottom. It stood, leaning to one side, with an object in its hand pointed toward the floor. She that thought maybe it was a gun, but she couldn't be sure.

She panicked and attempted to move an arm to alert her boyfriend, who slept only a few inches away, but she felt paralyzed. Tensing every muscle in her body, willing anything to move, she passed out. The fatigue and blackness that overcame her made her feel like she was going under anesthesia. Later, she jolted awake, scared and confused. The bedroom was dark, the shadow gone and everything was back to normal. It seemed as if whatever it was wanted her to know that it was in the house and in control.

Middle-of-the-night encounters with a ghost at the bottom of the bed and the person unable to move are common. Scientific explanations suggest that the mind wakes at some point during the night, but the body stays asleep. Most people who experience these bedside apparitions are not convinced of the scientific explanation.

A few blocks down, also on Fifth Street, in the summer of 2015, three-year-old Blake* woke from a midday nap. He looked above the headboard of his parents' bed and smiled widely.

"Oh! It's the boy!" he exclaimed.

Blake then began rolling around on the bed as if he were imitating a boy above the bed. His mother, confused, didn't see anything on the wall whatsoever. He continued to laugh and interact with whatever he saw for a couple of minutes. His mother asked questions, but she never got a clear answer. Her son indicated that the boy had brown hair and a hat. He had seen the boy before and even knew his name, but years later, the mother could not recall what it was. She thought that the name was unusual and said it started with a D. If it was an apparition of a boy that Blake saw that day, it brought him a lot of joy.

27
Residual Hauntings
Fifth and Sixth Streets

A residual haunting is a supernatural experience that seems to replay at various times, often reenacting some time from the past. A possible example of this happened on Fifth Street, when a three-year-old boy stopped jumping on a trampoline in his backyard and hollered for his mother to look at the roof of their house. He pointed and said, "A man fell!" After repeating it a couple of times, he went back to jumping. This caused a moment of pause for the young woman because, shortly after moving in, a neighbor informed her that a previous owner had a heart attack while working on the roof and fell off. She never gave it another thought until that moment.

One block over, on Sixth Street, Jennifer Summers moved into a small apartment in 1994. She placed her mattress on the floor in the bedroom in what she determined must have been the same spot as all the previous tenants, based on the layout of the room. It wasn't long before she was awakened in the middle of the night by something that she could not see. When she tried to reposition herself, she felt a force pinning her feet down to the bed. She couldn't draw her legs up toward herself or roll over, no matter how hard she tried.

Jennifer didn't have pets or any other reasonable explanation for why her feet would have been trapped in that position. As she became more awake, she looked down to the bottom of the bed but saw nothing. After a moment or two, the weight gradually lifted, releasing her feet, and then disappeared altogether. She fell back to sleep and didn't feel the strange weight on her feet again that night or any other night.

The event was all but forgotten until, one day, a conversation with her coworkers revealed where she lived. Her coworkers not only knew the previous tenant of the apartment but were at his party the night that he died. They told her that the previous tenant wasn't feeling well and went to his bedroom to rest. He had been sitting with his face in his hands and his elbows on his knees toward the foot of the bed when he slumped off, dead. He had died of liver failure. Coincidently, this was the same spot where Jennifer felt her feet pinned down.

She didn't have any reason to doubt her coworkers' account of the events. They provided many details about the night, the location of furniture and how the man went from throwing a party to dying in the bedroom, including the condition of his yellowing skin. Jennifer believes his spirit continues to occupy that spot.

28

Someone Is in the House

Fifth Street

Joanna Lange* owns a large, three-story home on Fifth Street that was built in 1910. It was divided into apartments at some point, but when Joanna purchased the home with her husband in 1980, they reverted the house back into a single-family home. At first, the family didn't notice anything unusual, except for a few complaints from their teenage daughters about detached noises coming from the upstairs. They heard things like disconnected footsteps or balls bouncing down the stairs but weren't able to find anyone or anything when they checked for the source.

Through the years, Joanna's kids grew up and moved out. Then her husband passed away in 2013. She had to get used to living in the large house alone. She quit using the upstairs area, except for the occasional sewing project or guests when family came to visit. For peace of mind, her kids set up a wireless security alert system in the kitchen by the door. An infrared sensor detected motion that triggered a mechanism to chime in her bedroom. She thought she would sleep better with the security system, and at first, she did. Before long, however, the chime began going off in the middle of the night. Joanne found herself creeping around the house, trying to figure out what triggered the chime. It happened so many times that she finally quit using the system. One time, the chime woke her during a snowstorm, and she knew that if someone had come through the door, there would be snow on the rug, but it was dry. Curiously, she never experienced a false chime during the day.

A historic home in Baraboo. *Courtesy of Pam Thompson.*

Joanna believes her husband is still in the house, watching over her, and that's fine by her if he walks around, checking the doors at night. Once in a while, she even feels a brush of her hair as she sleeps. She began to wonder if it was her imagination.

One day, Joanna heard a loud bang on the floor above her as she sat in the living room. She slowly walked up the stairs and through the rooms. As she walked past the bathroom, she saw that the faucet was running. One of the grandkids must have left it on when they visited a few days before. She continued to investigate and eventually discovered that all of the board games had fallen off of a shelf in the closet. The shelf was still up, but the games, which had been up there for years, had fallen onto the floor. She wondered if it was her husband's way of telling her to get upstairs and turn the faucet off.

In 2016, Joanna's sixteen-year-old granddaughter moved in and slept in an upstairs bedroom next to the attic door. One afternoon, while she was home alone, the granddaughter heard a creaking up the stairs and thought her grandmother was home until the shadow of an adult female walked past her bedroom door. Then it walked past again, a couple more times. Scared, the granddaughter closed her bedroom door, called her mother and turned the volume of the TV up until someone came home. This confirmed that there was definitely someone else in the house, possibly in addition to her husband, and it was attached to the upstairs area. They eventually named the spirit Lorraine for lack of anything else to call it. They were not afraid and continued about their business with little thought of her, although Joanne's other grandchildren refused to go upstairs.

29

Women in the Home

Ash Street

Ash Street was one of the most prominent streets in Baraboo in the late 1800s. Prestigious families built elaborate houses with front porches and decorative details. People often chatted with the property owners from the sidewalk during their evening constitutional. Originally called Bridge Street, in the late 1800s, the name was changed to Ash Street, due to the numerous ash trees that line the street. Today, some of the oldest and most decorated homes in Baraboo remain on this Street.

In 2003, Dana Walkman* parked her car across from a friend's house on Ash Street. As she got out of her car, she noticed a young woman who was no more than twenty years old standing in the doorway of her friend's house. Dana had never seen her before but thought it was one of the young women who lived in the house. The woman had straight blond hair that stretched down to her waist. As the woman stood in the doorway, she seemed to be looking down Ash Street, toward the river. The woman turned to look at Dana as she approached and then disappeared. Dana knocked when she arrived at the front door and discovered that no one was home. Dana entered the empty house and waited for her friend to return.

Growing up, Dana thought ghosts were scary, though she'd never actually seen one. Now that she had, she was not frightened at all. In fact, she immediately knew the woman wasn't real and was surprised to discover that she barely cared.

A few years later, Dana's daughter had the opportunity to move into the house. Dana and her daughter planned to meet one evening, but her daughter was running late, so Dana waited for her inside. From the couch in the living room, Dana glanced toward the foyer, through the French doors, and saw a young woman looking out the door in the entryway. The woman's back was to Dana, but she had dark, wavy, shoulder-length hair, similar to her daughter's hair. Dana immediately got up and walked toward the entryway, but the woman disappeared after only three steps. Perhaps the image was a result of shadows or a trick of the light, but Dana insists it looked like a young woman standing in the foyer.

After the second incident, Dana spoke to the owner of the house about her experiences. Unsurprised, he said that sometimes, at night, he would feel the sensation of someone sitting on the edge of the bed next to him. He always felt that it was a woman, and he was not afraid of her.

30

The Walker

Carpenter Street

Sometime in 2014, a resident on Carpenter Street woke in the middle of the night in an upstairs bedroom of her two-story home. She heard someone walking around her bedroom. She lay in bed with her eyes closed, thinking perhaps she was dreaming, but the sound continued. The wooden floorboards creaked as the person scurried over to one side of the room, stopped and then took a few more steps. The sound continued, getting farther away, then coming closer again. This went on for some time, but she could not physically see anyone in the room.

Eventually, she sat up and opened her eyes, putting her feet on the floor. She followed the sound with her eyes, as it seemed to go out into the hallway. The footsteps were ordinary and did not seem urgent, scared or sneaky. It sounded like someone had a lot of work to do, perhaps a housewife taking care of business, making the beds, tidying up the drawers, dusting and cleaning the windows.

She refers to the spirit as the Walker, since she has only experienced the sound of footsteps. The Walker would wake her multiple nights in a row and continue intermittently throughout the years, usually in the early morning hours between 3:00 and 4:00 a.m. Her husband, a heavy sleeper, has not heard the footsteps, but her kids have. They typically blame it on another family member because they are too young to realize that everyone is still in bed. This secretly validates her experience.

31

THE PHANTOM PRANKSTER

FIRST STREET

First Street in Baraboo was called Bench Street until 1890, as its position on the hill above the Baraboo River resembled a bench. It is located between the commercial and industrial historical centers of Baraboo. Martin Green* didn't believe in ghosts until 1995, when he moved into an apartment on First Street after accepting a job in a nearby town. He was a science teacher and had never been afraid to walk around in the dark. He soon discovered that logical explanations for things are sometimes elusive.

Martin moved into the affordable apartment with his wife and two-month-old black lab mix. Since the puppy was not house-trained, he bought a baby gate to keep it on the linoleum floor in the kitchen when they were not at home. The puppy was only about ten inches tall, so he thought it would work, but he found the puppy on the living room sofa when he got home the first day. The gate had not held the dog, but it wasn't knocked over. He wondered if the little dog had crawled or jumped over it. He purchased another baby gate and put it in the doorway above the other gate. Together, the gates reached a level close to six feet high. Satisfied, he went to work the next day. On his return, he found the dog on the couch again and the plants dumped all over the floor. The gates were still tight in the doorway. He yanked on them—they were rock-solid and would not budge.

The next day, the same thing happened. The one-foot-tall dog somehow navigated over double baby gates that were close to six feet high. This time, the plants were not only knocked over, but it looked like the puppy had skidded across the dirt, too. He went out and bought a dog kennel. It was plastic but sturdy.

In the meantime, Martin's landlord allowed him to fix the peeling wallpaper and cracks in the plaster in the stairwell leading upstairs. The project took multiple days, but he hoped it would be a great improvement to the stairwell. He broke off loose plaster, tore down the wallpaper and then plastered over the wall. One morning, he walked downstairs, admiring his handiwork, and noticed a word on the new plaster, high above the stairs.

HATE

It was spelled out in all capital letters that were about a quarter of an inch tall. It looked like it was written in pencil. Martin was taller than his wife. Hanging on the wall, reaching out in full height, he couldn't reach the word without standing on something. She was afraid of ladders, so it couldn't have been her. He asked her anyway to see if there was something they needed to talk about, but she was also confused about how it could have gotten there.

As Martin continued to puzzle over the strange incidents in the house, a previous tenant stopped by with the handle cranks for the windows, which she had accidentally packed while moving out. Martin learned that she had lived in the house for a few years and that strange things had happened to her and her animals as well. She had found out from a neighbor that an elderly man had died in the house from alcohol abuse, but no one was sure if this person could have been the cause of the supernatural activity.

As time went by, Martin and his family settled into the apartment. He put a workout bench in the smaller bedroom upstairs. He became curious about an attic hatch on the ceiling of the room. Old houses in Baraboo often have scuttle attics to provide access to the attic. The hatches were typically built in inconspicuous locations in the ceilings, easily reached with a ladder. Martin wondered if something might have been left in the attic over the years, so he grabbed his ladder and climbed up. He pushed and pushed on the two-by-three-foot panel, but it would not budge. He gave up and put the ladder away. A couple of nights later, Martin and his wife were awakened in the middle of the night by a loud bang. He immediately thought someone was breaking into the house. So, he grabbed his bat and walked around the entire house, looking for the culprit. He was sure he was going to find someone at the front door, back door or even the basement. He found no one. Without a doubt, the noise had come from somewhere inside the house, so he walked up and down the hall, checking the bathroom and his weight room. He realized that the panel from the attic had fallen to the floor, and it was propped against his weight bench with other debris around it from the attic.

Martin questioned his wife, asking if she had climbed up to the ceiling to mess with the panel above his weight bench, but again, she hadn't even noticed that there was a hatch in the ceiling. Martin grabbed his ladder to put the panel back up in the ceiling. He wasn't able to gently rock it into place like a drop ceiling–type tile; rather, he had to literally turn it on end, rotate it diagonally, push it up through the hole and let it drop back down. It could not have just fallen out. It would have to have been lifted up, rotated and turned diagonally in order to fall on the weight bench in the middle of the night. Martin recalled, "I'm a science teacher. I don't like it when things don't make sense."

A few months later, Martin backed his truck into the driveway in order to carry a few things into the house. He put the truck in gear, turned it off and locked the doors. He was always careful with his 1981 Chevy short bed truck with a three-speed transmission. It was jet black, and he had recently put in a new engine. He loved that thing and had only owned it for a year. He made a trip to the house and came back out to get more items. When he came out a third time, the truck was gone. It had jumped out of gear, rolled down the hill and hit the garage. He never had trouble with that transmission before or after. The truck wasn't even parked on a slant; he had it on the top of the hill as level as he could get it. If anything, it should have rolled into the street.

Time went by, and Martin's dog was growing up and turning into a friendly, well-mannered dog. She never barked or growled, except when someone would take a bath. The apartment did not have a shower; instead, it had a tub with an adapter spray nozzle to wash hair. Sometimes, Martin felt like maybe someone was watching him, but he was the only one home. The dog would sit next to the tub and stare out into the hallway, no matter how many times Martin tried to shoo her away. Eventually, the hair on the back of the dog's neck would stand up, and she would start growling. Then she'd get up and act like she was going to go after something. This was the only time the dog ever acted like that. Martin was not easily spooked, but that freaked him out because his dog did this on a fairly regular basis.

The purchase of the plastic kennel proved to be fairly successful in containing the dog during the day—that is, until one afternoon when Martin got home, and the dog met him at the door. He looked at the kennel and saw that the vertical slits on the upper right side had been cut to make a triangular escape route. Martin looked over the kennel for quite some time.

It did not look like the plastic was chewed, as there were no bite marks. It looked as if someone had taken a dull knife and cut it. Even then, Martin wasn't entirely sure that the dog could fit through the little hole that had been cut into the side of the kennel until he put the dog back in and enticed her out with all the treats he had. The dog did manage to shimmy through the hole, but that still didn't explain how the kennel was cut. He couldn't figure out why she would want to get out of the kennel anyway. It was her safe place. Sometimes, the dog would sleep in the kennel while he and his wife watched TV. It seemed to him that something was messing with his dog. Martin went through a list of people in his head who could have done it. The landlord lived out of town and never stopped by, the neighbor didn't have a key, the apartment doors were not broken into and his wife, again, was just as confused as he was.

The freakiest memory Martin had of the apartment on First Street was the day he moved out. His mother-in-law helped them carry everything to the U-Haul, and then they all drove to the new house separately. Before Martin got into his truck, he looked back at the apartment and saw someone standing in the upper bedroom window. The venetian blinds were split about four inches, and a man with a darker skin tone looked out at him. He could only see the man's face from his eyebrows to his nose and the fingers that held down the blinds. Martin didn't mention the man in the window to anyone and was just happy to be leaving.

A few months later, Martin found out that his mother-in-law had also seen the man standing in the bedroom window as they drove away. He was commenting on how much he liked the new house because it was more comfortable, strange things weren't happening all the time and the dog had settled down. That's when his mother-in-law described the man in the bedroom window, holding down the blinds, watching them leave.

Plenty of people moved in and out of the apartment over the years, some with no paranormal experiences and others with odd experiences. Twenty years later, Gina Whitman*, a stay-at-home mom, moved in with her husband, toddler and newborn baby. She remembered wondering why the rent was unusually low, but they desperately needed a larger apartment and didn't ask many questions. It wasn't long before her toddler began staring into the corners of the rooms and babbling about things they had never discussed with her. One day, her daughter said the word *ghost* and appeared to be talking about someone else in the room. They had never talked to her about ghosts, and Gina was with her all of the time, so she didn't know where this was coming from. Still, it wasn't impossible that her daughter could have learned the word from somewhere else or from TV, but her strange behavior always caused a moment of pause.

Other inexplicable things continued to happen in the apartment. Lights would flicker downstairs after they had been turned out for the night. The bathroom light often got turned on after Gina checked and double-checked that it was turned off. From the bottom of the stairs, they heard footsteps walking in the upper hallway when nobody was upstairs.

Gina had an automobile puzzle for the kids that would make the sound of the vehicle when the correct piece was put in the correct place. She never put batteries in the puzzle and left it in the closet with the pieces in a Ziploc bag until the kids were old enough to use it. At random times, the puzzle made vehicle noises on its own. She would hear the firetruck, police car and helicopter throughout the day and night. By this time, she quit trying to make sense of the strange things happening in the house, and she wouldn't even go and check it out.

She described a heavy feeling in the house, particularly in the smaller upstairs bedroom (with the scuttle attic) and the stairwell leading to the basement, where she would only go as far as the ripped, green, flowered wallpaper before stopping. She described it like someone was sitting on her chest and she couldn't breathe. Soon, Gina's relationship with her husband began to suffer. They fought a lot and knew they had to get out of the apartment, but they had few options since they had little money and had signed a lease.

On Halloween, Gina dressed her two-year-old daughter in a purple monster costume, which the little girl loved and wore around the house a number of times. That day, however, her daughter started screaming and crying when she looked in the mirror, and she tried to pull the costume off her shoulder. She refused to wear it. That night, the ghost came to her husband in a dream and told him that he had put his hand on her shoulder while she looked in the mirror. He didn't mean to scare her.

PART V

Country Ghosts—Stories Within a Ten-Mile Radius of Baraboo

32

The Returning Picture

Highway 33

One leading theory among folks who don't want to live in a haunted house is that a brand-new house should be ghost-free. It just stands to reason that spirits are commonly known to inhabit buildings that they frequented when they were alive, so to avoid ghosts, one must live in a house without a history. That would work, in theory, if it weren't for the fact that the property on which a house is built almost certainly has a history. Many new houses are built on properties that have clear evidence of past inhabitation, such as old foundations, windmills or outbuildings. While visiting his girlfriend's house on Highway 33, Jesse Miller* discovered that ghosts can and will occupy a new house.

Jesse first visited the house in 2010, when he and Raina* started dating during his junior year of high school. Her family built the home in the 1990s and have been the sole owners. Jesse and Raina watched a scary movie in the large basement on their first date. In addition to a TV room, the basement also had a laundry room and a workshop. The workshop was previously used as a bedroom by one of Raina's brothers before he moved to college. Raina fell asleep just as the action ramped up in the movie. Jesse looked over at the workshop door and saw that it was open. This gave him an ominous feeling. He didn't remember it being open but supposed it could have been. He went back to watching the movie, then aware of the open door. Something caught his eye, and he looked back over; there stood an apparition of a little girl, probably around six years old, in the doorway. She wore a white dress and had shoulder-length blond hair. He initially thought she was solid, but

Old foundations are common in rural areas and serve as evidence of past inhabitation. *Courtesy of Mary Farrell-Stieve.*

when he focused on her, he realized he could see through her and that she had a slight glow. She smiled and shrugged her shoulders. Jesse shook Raina to wake her up, taking his eyes off the little girl for just a second, and when he looked back, she was gone.

Jesse quickly forgot about the little girl in the basement until Raina's older brothers came home a year later and brought up the topic of ghost stories. Jesse told them that he saw a little girl in their basement, and both brothers looked at him in amazement and said, "You saw her, too?"" They compared stories and determined that they all saw the same apparition in the house and had similar experiences, except the brothers had also heard a child's laughter from time to time.

The little girl wasn't the only ghost in the house. When the oldest brother, Jake*, had his bedroom in the basement, he often felt a weight on his bed while he slept, as if someone was sitting on the mattress. One time, he woke in the middle of the night and went up to the kitchen for a glass of water. As he stepped up onto the main floor, he saw the apparition of a tall man in a suit standing in front of the refrigerator. The man didn't move when Jake entered. Spooked, Jake backstepped down the hallway, toward his sister Raina's bedroom. He found her sitting straight up in bed, looking at him as he came into view. He said her name, but she seemed to be asleep. He said her name again and asked what she was doing, but she lay back down before answering. He looked back over to the refrigerator, and the man was gone.

Then there was the painting in the basement that another brother, Logan*, found while visiting for Easter. Apparently, it was right under the stairs, but no one had ever seen it before, even though they had combed through the entire basement many times. He took a picture of the painting and sent it to Jesse because it was creepy. They laughed, but there was something familiar about the painting—like Jesse had seen it before. Later that night, Jesse looked at the picture again and realized that the little girl in the painting was the same little girl he had seen in the basement. After that, Logan asked his mom to get rid of the painting, which she did. A month later, Logan received a text from his father containing a picture of the same painting. The painting had somehow returned to the house. The family gave the painting away again, and it has not come back.

These ghostly encounters inspired the family to purchase introductory ghost hunting equipment. They set up a camera in the basement bedroom where the little girl had been seen and placed Jesse's laptop on a table by the TV to feed all of the microphones, which were placed near the TV, the workshop, the stairway and the laundry room. Their objective was to record whatever they could.

The four decided to start their hunt in the laundry room, which was the largest, darkest area in the basement. They each stood quietly in a different corner of the room, knowing that their eyes would never adjust to the darkness. The room contained shelves of tools, the washer and dryer and many other things that were haphazardly placed in the middle. After about ten minutes of silence, they tried provoking the spirit, saying things like, "If you are out there, do something."

Nothing happened immediately. Then something tipped over in the middle of the room. They continued to provoke the spirit. Something crashed into the tool shelf above Jesse's head, causing a wrench to fall off and land on the floor next to him, nearly missing his head. Afraid someone was going to get hurt, Logan flipped on the light switch, and everyone was still standing in their respective corners.

Then they heard a crash in the TV room, and everyone ran to see what it was. Jesse's laptop was upside-down on the floor. He had placed it four inches from the edge of the table, a place it could not have fallen from on its own. The entire hard drive was shot. All of the audio recordings were destroyed. They wondered if the spirit had intentionally broken the computer because it had recorded something it wasn't supposed to or if the spirit was trying to prove a point. Jesse took the hard drive out in an attempt to recover the data. He kept the hard drive through the years but has never been able to recover anything from it. It is more dead than any hard drive he has ever seen. They have not gone back to record.

33
Bygone Travelers
Hogsback Road

Seeing an apparition in period clothing is often a bewildering experience, especially if it's in a new house. In 1992, Amber Rice* and her husband built a home on Hogsback Road. It wasn't long before their daughter complained of waking in the middle of the night to see two children, a boy and a girl, dressed in period clothes and standing at the end of her bed. They may never know exactly who the children are or why they are attached to the land, but one possible explanation is that the house was built near the original stagecoach route to the area, dating back more than 150 years.

When Prescott Brigham drove the first stagecoach to Sauk County in 1844, observers flocked to the Western Hotel in downtown Baraboo just to get a glimpse. His four horses had just pulled a Concord-style stagecoach through the difficult terrain of the Baraboo Bluffs. By 1854, A.H. Clark had established a triweekly stagecoach line that wound through the northern bluffs between Reedsburg and Baraboo. The stagecoach took approximately four hours to travel between the two communities and stopped at a halfway point near Hogsback Road. It is uncertain whether the halfway point was a house or a tavern. This stagecoach route continued to run until the train connected the two communities in 1871.

Apparitions continue to appear in the house to this day, but they don't seem to do more than make themselves known. One evening, Amber went into her bedroom and used the light from the hallway to cast light into her room. As she walked past her bed, she saw the outline of a person. She excused herself on her way past, thinking it was her husband, but then she realized it could not have been her husband because he wasn't home. When she looked back to see who it was, the room was empty.

Another time, Amber saw, out of the corner of her eye, a boy run down the hallway, toward the bedrooms. He was wearing summer clothes, and she specifically remembered seeing bare arms and legs. She thought it was odd because she had just left her son in the basement. She checked the bedrooms, and they were empty. Her son was, in fact, still in the basement.

34
Something Is Out There
Man Mound Road

Strange sounds are sometimes heard in the forests around Baraboo. Witnesses have described a cross between a roar and a howl deriving from some place out of sight. Many suggest it is inhuman, and others say it sounds more human than animal. Some people even speculate that bigfoot is responsible. Others won't go that far but admit that something is out there—something that isn't normal. Whatever it is, many people around the Baraboo Bluffs claim to have heard the sounds and think that whatever is causing it may have been around for centuries.

Amelia Cotter encountered an unidentifiable sound at Man Mound County Park in December 2018. The sound didn't have anything to do with the mound, but it originated in the woods next to it. She'd just arrived in town, and at mid-morning, she and her husband drove on icy roads out to the unique effigy mound. A blanket of snow covered the ground. When they arrived, the parking lot was free of tire tracks and footprints; it was clear that no one had been there in days.

They were immediately able to discern where the mound was located under the snow and where, decades before, the legs had been cut off by the road. Man Mound is a human-shaped effigy mound that is 214 feet long by 48 feet wide. It is the only human-shaped mound left in the United States and has been preserved at Man Mound County Park since 1908. The mound was placed in the National Register of Historic Places in 1978 and was designated a National Historic Landmark in 2016. Many who visit recognize the site as a sacred space.

As the couple got out of the car to take pictures, Amelia immediately felt like things weren't right. She wouldn't describe herself as sensitive, but she just felt like something was off. The air was dead quiet, and no one was around. The park is three miles from Baraboo on a sparsely populated road. They walked around the mound and soon heard a high-pitched shrieking from the woods. It was a piercing sound, not like any animal they had ever heard. Whatever it was moved closer, but strangely, it was not accompanied by the sound of footsteps or rustling trees. All of the leaves had fallen for the winter, so they could see a good distance through the woods. The shrieking sounded close, but they could not see whatever was causing it. The sound seemed to come from everywhere at once and nowhere in particular.

They quickly finished up and got back into the car. If it was an animal, they didn't want to encounter it. They felt like something didn't want them there. With sweaty hands, her husband tried to start the rental car, but it wouldn't start. They attempted to call for help, but their cellphones were out of the service area. They felt stuck.

Amelia went to the side of the road to attempt to flag down the next car, but she hadn't seen a car drive by since they had arrived. The shrieking bellowed from the forest again. It happened a total of three times. Finally, a car drove by. It slowed as she waved but continued past before eventually turning around. The occupants, an older couple, rolled down the window an inch so that Amelia could explain their predicament. The older man was able to start their car almost immediately and then went on his way.

Amelia and her husband took a second to collect themselves and then backed up the car to pull out. They thought perhaps their imaginations had run wild and that they had made a big deal out of nothing. Then they heard a *bump, bump, bump* on the rear passenger window. It sounded like someone tapping on it. Amelia expected to turn around and see the man who had just helped them—except she had just watched him get into his car and drive away. But when she looked, there was nobody around. The parking lot was just as vacant as it had been when they arrived. She felt like it was a "gotcha" moment by whatever was in the woods that had caused their uneasiness.

35

Church Road and Saint Michael's Lutheran Cemetery

Lewiston Township, Columbia County

Ten miles from Baraboo as the crow flies, Saint Michael's Lutheran Cemetery is tucked in the hillside off of Church Road. Many high schoolers make their way there because of its reputation as a local paranormal hotspot. Local legend suggests a girl hanged herself from a branch near the cemetery, and her apparition can be seen, at times, hanging from a tree. It is also said that the rope can be heard swinging in the wind, and the branch can be heard breaking under her weight. Regardless of whether that story is true, the paranormal activity in this secluded area has been featured online and in books. Witnesses report experiencing apparitions, disconnected voices and the manipulation of their senses. Church Road dead ends just beyond the cemetery, and it is unclear if the cemetery or the road has more activity. One thing is certain: after getting their drivers' licenses, it is almost a rite of passage for teenagers to borrow their family cars to cruise out to Church Road with friends to see if anyone can glimpse a ghost.

With so much interest in this secluded cemetery, the public is asked to be respectful. Many people who still live in the Lewiston Township have relatives buried in the cemetery. Church Road is also surrounded by private property. The cemetery is closed from dusk to dawn, and police will ticket anyone loitering on the road at night. Special permission is granted by the Lewiston Township, on occasion, for after-hours explorations, provided there are no shenanigans.

The view down Church Road. *Courtesy of Pam Thompson.*

Saint Michael's Lutheran Church stood on the site from 1859 to 1927. The church building is no longer there, but the cemetery, containing approximately sixty graves, remains in the churchyard. Burials are no longer allowed at the cemetery, and the Lewiston Township takes care of its maintenance. Sadly, vandals knocked over some of the oldest headstones a few years ago. Many have been set back up, but they are broken beyond repair and unreadable.

In 2015, high schoolers Dawson Hinz and Steven Mordini found their way to the cemetery after a friend sent a Snapchat photograph from the cemetery, which inaccurately posted the date as 1864. No one can explain how that happened. Steven's mother told him he could not go. She was sensitive and knew nothing good could come of it. He went anyway, saying he'd be at Dawson's house. The friends invited a couple of people along and intended to stay on the road, close to the car, to take pictures. If it went well, they would try to talk to the spirits.

By the time they got to the small hill on Church Road, Steven had a weird feeling and didn't want to go any farther. Having never been there before, the boys did not know that this was the location of the cemetery. They soon crept along the short distance to the end of the road and got out of the car.

Dawson immediately heard a branch break in a tree as he stepped out onto the road. Then his phone malfunctioned. It kept flashing as if it was taking a picture, but it never actually captured one. While he fumbled with his phone, a friend got a picture that sent her running back to the truck. The photograph was taken at night and is of poor quality, but it showed something hanging from the tree in front of them. Whatever was there, it appeared to have blond hair and a blue dress—its head leaning to one side.

They all got back into the car and drove away, but Dawson struggled in other ways. He kept telling himself that they were out having fun, but he battled feelings of sadness, anger and hatred, dark, empty feelings that were not his own, almost as if something was manipulating his feelings or controlling his thoughts. He was overwhelmed with eye-watering emotion that lasted most of the way back to town.

The next day, Steven made a quick stop at home to change before work. Before long, he received a text from his mother, indicating that she knew where he had been the night before. Steven confronted his friends, asking which of them had told his mother that he'd been at the cemetery, but no one had told her. When he got home, he found out that his mother had discovered the spirit of a little boy on the front step of their house, apparently waiting for Steven. The spirit told her that he was from the cemetery and had sat between Steven and a blond girl in the back seat of the car. She told the spirit to go back to the cemetery.

Steven returned to Church Road one more time a few nights later because his father, a nonbeliever, wanted to see it. Slightly spooked, they geared up with sage, just in case the spirits really could tag along on the way home. They planned to leave the truck running and doors open to ward off any problems that might prevent their departure.

Standing at the end of the road, Steven's father instantly heard voices in the forest. It sounded like a group of people moving down a path, toward them. Steven could not hear the voices and assured his father that there were no paths for them to be moving down. Moments later, Steven sat on the bumper of his truck and quickly developed a bad headache and nausea. He described the sudden onset of physical illness as "internally awful" and "eye-watering." It came on unexpectedly, similar to the emotional strife that had engulfed Dawson a week before. Perhaps whatever the spirit might have been going through was transferred to them. As they returned to the truck and drove away, Steven felt worse. He didn't start feeling better until they stopped a few miles down the road to regroup.

36

The Old Highway 12 Hitchhiker

Business Highway 12

Imagine driving down Highway 12 at night near Baraboo when, suddenly, a man appears on the side of the road in the farthest reaches of your headlights. He's wearing army greens, a backpack and a hat. He has dark, shoulder-length hair and is walking with an unusual gait. That is how witnesses describe their initial encounter with an apparition known as the Highway 12 Hitchhiker. Witnesses observe him in such detail that there is no reason to believe he isn't real. The apparition does not hold out a thumb to flag down cars. Most experience a mixture of surprise and concern as they drive by because the man is on the wrong side of the road, in the dark and a little too close to traffic.

Then a mile down the road, they see him again—same guy, same clothes, same unusual gait. The Highway 12 Hitchhiker is so well known that the story has been featured on TV and in numerous books. People have reported sightings so often that, for a while, a website was set up to collect information on him. Still, no one knows who this man was or why he walks Highway 12 at night. There are no tragic stories of a man getting hit by a car on that stretch of road.

The apparition is seen on the original stretch of Highway 12, before the State of Wisconsin rerouted and expanded sections of the highway around Baraboo. The highway is now either wider than the original road or has been moved entirely, renamed and even dead ends at one point. Today, the original Highway 12 can be found on parts of the four-lane highway between Sauk City and Baraboo. The rest has been renamed Business 12,

Highway BD and Highway 136 through Baraboo to Lake Delton.

Many people wonder what the change in highway structure means for the hitchhiker. Jacob Carignan found out the answer to this question while traveling down Business 12 with three friends. The story starts on a dark and foggy night in the spring of 2019. The four friends drove back from Lake Delton in an older vehicle, after an evening of failed plans. Since they had some time to kill, Jacob told his friends the story of the Highway 12 Hitchhiker, and they soon planned to drive the old road to the dead end to see if they could see anything.

The road marker of this notoriously haunted highway. *Courtesy of Pam Thompson.*

It should be noted that his friends did not believe in ghosts. They mocked the story. They laughed, and each jokingly pushed down the locks on the car doors "to keep the ghost out." It should also be noted that nothing in this car was automatic. The car was old.

As they drove along the highway through Baraboo and then out of town, heading toward the Skillet Creek intersection, Jacob saw something in the headlights up ahead but dismissed it as an animal. Within a couple of seconds, the headlights revealed a man in army green pants and a jacket, with shoulder-length hair and a backpack. Jacob kept quiet; his friends had not yet seen him, and he wasn't sure what he was seeing. They drove closer, and one of his friends shrieked; then the others panicked. The driver passed the man quickly, crossing the centerline to get around him. The hitchhiker outside was walking too close to traffic, just as the story indicated. Jacob turned to look out the window at the hitchhiker's face as the car passed, but it was too fast, and the door frame was in the way. They suspected the apparition would not appear again, as the road ended just under a mile away. Still, everyone in the car was very nervous.

Less than a mile ahead, the young men stopped the car at the end of the road. The new highway crossed on a bridge overhead, completely inaccessible to them. The only way back to town was past the apparition.

The dead end of old Highway 12, where the apparition of a hitchhiker is thought to still roam. *Courtesy of Pam Thompson.*

Suddenly, all four doors in the car unlocked at the same time, even though they were not automatic. This was just the motivation the boys needed. The trip back to town was much faster than the trip out.

37

SUDDENLY APPEARED

HIGHWAY T

It wasn't until Baraboo resident Chad Buchen took a downtown Baraboo haunted walk and learned about the Highway 12 Hitchhiker that he realized he had also seen a ghost along a Baraboo highway, but it wasn't the hitchhiker. Until that moment, he didn't realize apparitions could be seen outside in public. Many of the apparitions reported along highways remain a mystery. In Chad's case, he was driving with a friend along Highway T, toward Wisconsin Dells, in the fall of 2016. It was late in the evening. The apparition of a man suddenly appeared in the headlights along the side of the road, moments before they passed. Neither occupant of the car saw the man walking down the road or approach the road before his sudden appearance. The moon was bright that night and lit up the fields. They could see that the corn had already been cut for the season. The apparition stood on the right shoulder, facing the road, and wore blue military-type cargo pants with a white shirt. He stared straight ahead and did not move or flinch, despite being dangerously close to the car. In a delayed reaction, they both confirmed after passing that they had, in fact, seen a man on the road under bizarrely surprising circumstances. Chad believes he saw an apparition that night and has thought about the man's unexpected appearance on the road numerous times since.

BIBLIOGRAPHY

Apps, Jerold. *Ringlingville USA*. Madison: Wisconsin Historical Society Press, 2005.

Atkinson, Don. *Baraboo: A Selected History.* Bloomington, IN: Xlibris Corporation, 2008.

Axness, Anna Mae. "Wisconsin Death Records: Saint Michael's Lutheran Cemetery, Lewiston, Columbia County, Wisconsin." Interment.net Cemetery Records Online. September 22, 2016. www.interment.net.

Baraboo Centennial Committee. "A Century of Schools." Historical plaque located at the Baraboo Civic Center. Baraboo, WI. 1982.

———. "Indian Mounds and Village." Historical plaque located on the Baraboo River Walk. Baraboo, WI. 1982.

Baraboo News Republic. "C.A. Gollmar Succumbs to Heart Attack." February 21, 1929.

———. Obituary: Viola Mildred Putz. October 7, 1937.

Baraboo's Big Top Parade and Circus Celebration. "Baraboo's Rich Circus Heritage." www.bigtopparade.com.

Boyd-Jones, Veda. "Winnebago/Ho-Chunk." Updated September 18, 2020. www.encyclopedia.com.

Boyer, Dennis. *Driftless Spirits: Ghosts of Southwest Wisconsin*. Madison, WI: Prairie Oak Press. 1996.

Bromley, Ben. "Baraboo Eyes Depots Future." *Baraboo News Republic*, September 23, 2016. www.wiscnews.com.

———. "Ghost Light Returns to Ringling Stage." *Baraboo News Republic*, January 28, 2015. www.wiscnews.com.

Canfield, William H. *Outline Sketches of Sauk County, Including Its History from the First Marks of Man's Hand to 1891, and its Topography.* Vol. 2. Baraboo, WI: N.p., 1891.

Charles Ringling House. National Register of Historic Places registration form. May 21, 1997. www.npgallery.nps.gov.

Circus World Museum. "Ring Barn, 1901." Historical plaque located on the Ring Barn at Circus World Museum. Baraboo, WI.

———. "Winter Quarters Shops, 1910." Historical plaque located on Water Street. Baraboo, WI.

Cole, Harry Ellsworth. "The City of Baraboo." In *A Standard History of Sauk County, Wisconsin,* 423–68. New York: Lewis Publishing Company, 1918. www.baraboopubliclibrary.org.

———. *Stagecoach and Tavern Days in the Baraboo Region.* Whitefish, MT: Kessinger Legacy Reprints, January 1, 1926.

Coleman, Loren. *Mysterious America*. New York: Gallery Books, 2007.

Cotter, Amelia. *Where the Party Never Ended: Ghosts of the Old Baraboo Inn*. North Ridge, OH: Haunted Road Media LLC, 2021.

Cullison, Dean. *A Sauk County Railtown Tour Along the Chicago & North Western Railroad Right of Way*. Baraboo, WI: DD Publishing, D&D Associates, 2003.

Daley, Jason. "Get to Know Man Mound, One of 10 New National Historic Landmarks." *Smithsonian Magazine*, November 11, 2016. www.smithsonianmag.com.

De Laruelle, Scott. "Visiting a Local Haunt." *Baraboo News Republic*, October 31, 2003.

Devil's Lake State Park. "Rocks and Water through the Ages." Revised October 4, 2017. www.dnr.wi.gov.

Dewel, Robert "Bob" C. "The 1870s." In *Sauk County and Baraboo.* Vol. 1. Baraboo, WI: Sauk County Historical Society and the UW Extension Arts and Culture Committee, 2009. www.baraboopubliclibrary.org.

———. "Genteel Baraboo and the Bloody South: Tales of Earlier Days." In *Sauk County and Baraboo*. Vol. 4. Baraboo, WI: Sauk County Historical Society and the UW Extension Arts and Culture Committee, 2013. www.baraboopubliclibrary.org.

Downtown Baraboo Historic District. National Register of Historic Places registration form. May 2, 2014. www.cityofbaraboo.com.

Earleywine, Betty. "Ringling Brothers in Broadhead." Brodhead Historical Society. www.brodheadhistory.org.

Endres, Susan. "Trio to Reminisce About Boo-U's Early Days at Public Lecture." *Baraboo News Republic*, May 6, 2019.

Erickson, Doug. "The Ghost of the Old Baraboo Inn, Many Years Ago the Restaurant Was a Brothel, and Recent Guests Have Reported Seeing Apparitions of a Woman Dressed as a Saloon Dancer." *Wisconsin State Journal*, July 5, 2005. www.madison.com.

Fitzpatrick, Laurence. "Transients Rounded up in Search for Mad Killer of Mrs. Alberta Gollmar." *Wisconsin State Journal*, September 23, 1938.

Food Network. "10 Most-Haunted Restaurants in America." Posted to YouTube on October 21, 2017. www.youtube.com.

French, H.E. "How Baraboo Streets Received Their Names." Sauk County Historical Society. August 16, 1917. www.saukcountyhistory.org.

Getsinger, Annie. "Wanna Buy a Ringling Mansion?" *Baraboo News Republic*, July 31, 2013. www.wiscnews.com.

Gollmar, Robert H. *My Father Owned a Circus*. Caldwell, ID: Caxton Printers Ltd., 1965.

Hesselburg, George. "The Extraordinary Life of the Ringlings' Sally." August 30, 2005. www.madison.com.

Hometown Horror. Season 1, episode 5, "Three-Ring Terror." Posted by Travel Channel to YouTube on December 2, 2019. www.youtube.com.

Klatt, Mary Beth. "Uncovering Ballroom Gems." *Realtor Magazine*, January 1, 2008. www.magazine.realtor.

Lamkin, Virginia. "Theatre 'Ghost Light' Superstitions." *Seeks Ghost*. March 5, 2013. www.seeksghosts.blogspot.com.

Lange, Kenneth I., and Ralph T. Tuttle. *A Lake Where Spirits Live.* 4th ed. In collaboration with the State of Wisconsin, Department of Natural Resources. Baraboo, WI: Bananaboat Advertising Graphics, 2007.

Lewis, Chad. *Paranormal Wisconsin Dells and Baraboo*. Sun Prairie, WI: On the Road Publications, 2018.

Lewis, Chad, and Terry Fisk. *The Wisconsin Road Guide to Haunted Locations*. Eau Claire, WI: Unexplained Research Publishing Company, 2004.

McDonald, Martha. "The Restoration of Al. Ringling Theatre by Isthmus Architecture." *Traditional Building*, Revised February 5, 2020. www.traditionalbuilding.com.

Mid-Continent Railway Museum. "A Town Called North Freedom." From *Whistle in the Wind*, MCRHS, 1997. Updated 2020. www.midcontinent.org.

Milwaukee Public Museum. "Ho-Chunk Oral Tradition." www.mpm.edu.

Montgomery, David, and Kelly McCullough. "Albert C. Ringling." Immigrant Entrepreneurship. August 22, 2018. www.immigrantentrepreneurship.org.

National Park Service. "Effigy Moundbuilders." Effigy Mounds National Monument. Updated April 14, 2017. www.nps.gov.

Natural Bridge State Park. Wisconsin State Park System. www.dnr.wi.gov.

Olson, Keri J. *Healing Presence, A History of Caring*. Baraboo, WI: Ballindalloch Press, 2012.

One Sauk, Naturally. "*Hoocąk Ciinąk Nį̨į Hooguc Hikįjąija*: Ho-Chunk Villages on the Baraboo River." Interpretive panel located on the Baraboo Riverwalk. Baraboo, WI.

———. "Mounds of the Baraboo Valley." Interpretive panel located on the Baraboo Riverwalk. Baraboo, WI.

Parker, Cedric. "Mrs. Gollmar, Victim of Brutal Murder, Trouped 2 Decades in Circus with Mate." *Capital Times*, September 24, 1938.

Prigge, Matthew J. "The Great Circus Parade: The History of a Uniquely Milwaukee Tradition." *Shepherd*, December 5, 2016. www.shepherdexpress.com.

Rhinelander Daily News. "Slayer of Baraboo Woman Shot, Killed." September 24, 1938. www.newspapers.com.

Ringling House Bed & Breakfast. "Relax, Rekindle & Relish." www.ringlinghousebnb.com.

Sauk County Historical Society. *Baraboo,* Postcard History Series. Charleston, SC: Arcadia Publishing, 2017.

———. "Reinking's Store and Ringling's Second Wardrobe Dept." Historical plaque located on Oak Street. Baraboo, WI. 1985.

Sauk County, Wisconsin. "Man Mound Park." www.co.sauk.wi.us.

Shrake, Peter. "The Circus City: An Overview of the Various Winter Quarters of Baraboo." *Bandwagon* 59, no. 4 (2015): 8–39.

———. "Where the Elephants Used to Roar: A Historical Sketch of Ringlingville's Elephant House." *Bandwagon* 61, no. 3 (2017): 38–45.

Spychalla, Craig. "Hip to Grow Hops: A Sauk County Man Is Uncovering Roots to the Area Hops." *Baraboo News Republic*, October 11, 2013.

Tallmadge Sainz, Menaine. "Exhibit Features Memories of Stand Rock Indian Ceremonial." *Madison 365*, July 19, 2018. www.madison365.com.

Tully, M. Richard. *The Phantom Finger and Other Ghost Stories from the Al. Ringling Theatre*. Baraboo, WI: Ballindalloch Press, 2014.

Waddel, Kathy. "Sauk County Reflections: 1938 Suspected Killer Shot Dead." *Baraboo News Republic*, September 16, 2013.

Ward, Joseph Wayne. *Baraboo Wisconsin 1850 to 2010, Chronology of the Growth of the Commercial & Retail Districts.* Vols. 1–5. Baraboo, WI: Joseph Wayne Ward, 2013. www.baraboopubliclibrary.org.

Wisconsin Historical Society. "Historical Essay: The Battle of Wisconsin Heights, 1832." www.wisconsinhistory.org.

———. "Property Record: 136 4th Ave" Al. Ringling Theatre. www.wisconsinhistory.org.

Witkowski, Monica. "Great Circus Parade." *Encyclopedia of Milwaukee.* 2016. www.emke.uwm.edu.

Wolter, Paul. "Al. Ringling Theatre: Centennial Tale." Al. Ringling Theatre. 2015. www.alringling.org.

———. "Circus Kings Castles: The Baraboo Homes of the Ringlings." *Bandwagon* 59, no. 4 (2015): 40–53.

Wydeven, Adrian. "The History of Wolves in Wisconsin." State of Wisconsin, Department of Natural Resources. May 18, 2011. www.dnr.wi.gov.

About the Authors

Shelley Mordini is described as adventurous, joyful and generous in the *Fabric of our Community* mural in downtown Baraboo. Shelley normally works as a high school special education teacher. She is also the owner of Baraboo Tours, a historic and haunted walking tour company in Baraboo, Wisconsin. Shelley enjoys showing people the legacy the Ringling Brothers left behind and talking about the ghost that put the *Boo* in Baraboo. Since purchasing a rickshaw to give tours, Shelley can often be seen whizzing around Baraboo, off to another adventure. Do you have a ghost story you would like to share about Baraboo? Contact Shelley at baraboootours@yahoo.com.

Gwen Herrewig enjoys nature, mysteries and a good story. She has worn many hats while traveling around, guiding tours of caves and glaciers and filling numerous office positions, supporting our natural resources. She recently conducted haunted walking tours of downtown Baraboo and interpretive paranormal experiences in haunted buildings. Gwen holds a master of science degree in natural resources with an emphasis in environmental education and interpretation. She lives with her family in Baraboo.